The Working Mother:

A SURVEY OF PROBLEMS AND PROGRAMS IN NINE COUNTRIES

Second Edition, Revised

ALICE H. COOK

New York State School of
Industrial and Labor Relations
Cornell University

Library of Congress Catalog Card Number: 78-620004
International Standard Book Number: 0-87546-067-4

ORDER FROM

Publications Division
New York State School of
Industrial and Labor Relations
Cornell University
Ithaca, New York 14853

Contents

Preface

In the three years that have passed since the first edition of *The Working Mother* appeared, more, and more recent, statistics on women's employment have become available. My assistant and I have tried to incorporate these new figures. In doing so, we note with interest an unlagging trend toward the employment of ever higher proportions of married women and mothers in the female work force in all the countries for which we have reasonably precise information. The need for attention to the special problems of the working mother has by no means diminished, nor have these problems been adequately recognized and met, so far as I can ascertain.

Several trips to Europe in 1975, 1976, and 1977 and one to Australia in 1976 in connection with a study on the place and problems of women in European trade unions have provided opportunity for maintaining contact with sources of information on the working mother. The text has been changed and corrected to include this up-to-date information.

For the important help that my assistant, Mary Cullen, has given me on the revisions I am deeply grateful. To the many correspondents and interview informants who have helped keep me up to date on the status of the working mother and programs of assistance designed to meet her need, my continuing thanks.

Alice H. Cook

Preface to the First Edition

This monograph is the first of a series of reports on a worldwide study of working mothers. With Ford Foundation support, in 1972 and 1973 I visited nine countries in order to acquaint myself with the working conditions of employed mothers, with national policies that might encourage or discourage their working, and with voluntary and state programs organized to offer them support.

The original plan was to visit four communist and four noncommunist countries; the plan had to be changed, however, because I was able to obtain visas only to three communist countries. Then in the course of travel I had the opportunity to add two noncommunist countries that were not included in my original itinerary. In the end I visited Sweden, Israel, East Germany, West Germany, Romania, Austria, Russia, Japan, and Australia in that order, following an orientation period at the International Labour Organisation in Geneva.

I selected these countries because I hoped to find in them legislated and voluntary programs that would have been tested by some experience and that might have some interest, perhaps even applicability, in the United States, and because I knew something about their history and social structure. I had lived and worked for considerable periods over twenty-five years in Germany and Austria, knew German, and hoped that my close knowledge of that language would stand me in good stead, as indeed it did, not only in the two Germanys and Austria but in Romania, Sweden, and Israel. Also, during my academic career I had spent considerable time in Japan studying its trade unions and particularly the labor relations system in its public sector. I was eager to learn more about its working women, about whom I knew very little indeed.

Of the countries selected, two were developing economies — Israel and Romania; the rest were industrialized nations with a high participation rate for women in the work force. My hope that they would have experimented with a variety of programs affecting women workers was fully realized.

The length of the visits varied somewhat. Visas to the communist countries were limited to three weeks, but I was able to spend five to fifteen weeks in other countries. In addition, I had a month in Hong Kong acquainting myself with materials on the People's Republic of China in preparation for a visit, which in the end did not take place.

Now a retired professor of industrial and labor relations, I was for many years a working mother and a single head of family. I chose to look at working mothers rather than at women generally because it seemed to me that the experience of the working mother concentrates and epitomizes problems that women generally have to face and that I would find in this group all the circumstances with which women have to cope in the world of work plus the handling of the additional burdens of housekeeping and child care.

It was clear to me even as I began the study that the number of married women in the work force was increasing very rapidly. As I moved into the study it was further clear that census data for the most part have not yet caught up with the phenomenon in all its dynamic. A significant structural change is going on in the labor market, occasioned not just by the increasing numbers and proportion of women workers but precisely by the entry of married women, who now in many countries make up more than half of the female labor force.

My method of gathering information was similar in each country. I endeavored first to acquaint myself with national policy and programs affecting working mothers by interviewing and collecting documentary and statistical material from at least three ministries: education, labor, and social welfare, under whatever names they might be functioning. In some countries I sought information at the ministerial level on laws affecting marriage and the family, taxation, housing, and consumer protection. Where it was appropriate I talked with persons having responsibility for the administration of labor market, adult education, child care, and related social welfare programs.

A second group of informants consisted of representatives of women's organizations, including particularly the trade unions; leaders of national women's movements; and women in high places in the political parties. From these people, I endeavored to get a critique of the official programs in operation. I wanted to know what they had on their agendas to propose as changes and improvements, and I wanted further to estimate, to the extent I could do so, the influence and power they possessed for actually bringing these changes about.

Finally, I visited many factories and offices, taking the opportunity to talk with working mothers themselves. Many of these interviews had to be very short and they were often carried out under considerable difficulty because of noise or the fact that women were working on moving belts or continuously operating machines. In these interviews I limited myself to two questions: "How do you manage?" and "What kind of help would you most like to have?" When there was time to do so, I enlarged on the first question to learn about how these women organized their daily lives — when they got up, what tasks had to be completed before work, what arrangements they made for the children, how they got to work, what had to be done at home at the end of the workday, what the shift schedule might be, how much help they got from husbands or children, and when they finally got to bed. In spite of the difficulties of interviewing under these circumstances, and often through an interpreter, the results were extremely helpful to me in forming an impression of the problems that most concerned these working mothers and the resources they can bring to bear on their solution.

Although my research methods were informal, I kept careful notes on interviews, dictating from my notes every night onto tape which was sent back to my excellent secretary in the United States, Ms. Danilee Spano. She transcribed the tapes, keyed the documents I collected to the tapes, and prepared file boxes, country by country, as the journey progressed. I kept a diary as well in which I recorded impressions and experiences outside the interviews. In most countries I conducted fifty or more interviews from which I gathered the statistical and documentary data which served to check or to generalize my personal impressions.

On my return to the United States in January 1974, I began the job of organizing these materials topically, and in this work I have had the first-rate assistance of Ms. Mary McGinnis as research associate. She and I have augmented the material I shipped home by drawing on the Cornell University libraries, by requesting my original sources for additional supplementary information, and by consulting with colleagues who are specialists in related fields. Among those who have been particularly helpful have been Professors Marjorie Galenson, Ethel Vatter, Tove Hammer, Robert Aronson, Robert McKersie, Nicholas Tavuchis, Jennie Farley, Frank Miller, and Urie Bronfenbrenner, and from the extension divisions of Cornell University, Barbara Wertheimer in labor relations and Natalie Crowe in human ecology. I am especially indebted to Susan Berresford, Bob Schrank, and many of their colleagues at the Ford Foundation for friendly comment and criticism when I reported there on my return. After my return the foundation continued its financial support of my ongoing research and writing.

Friends in the Women's Bureau of the United States Department of Labor and members of the Urban Research Institute have likewise shown their interest and offered information and suggestions. I am grateful to them and shall continue to turn to them when I need their help.

Not least generous have been the many newfound friends and colleagues who expedited my trip, shared their experiences and views and materials with me, offered hospitality, and have continued their interest and concern by correspondence. Among these I must especially mention Dr. Sylvia von Eltz and Marian Kärre of Stockholm; Rennie Lynne-Browne of the Women's Bureau of the Australian Ministry of Labour and Professor John Niland, formerly of the Australian National University and now at the University of New South Wales; in Japan, Ryoko Akamatsu of the Women's Bureau of the Ministry of Labor, Professor Hiroko Hiyashi of Kyushu University, and trade union women leaders from both Domei and Sohyo; in Israel, Aliza Tamir and Leah Brakin of Histadrut, the trade union federation, Professor Rivka Bar-Josef of the Hebrew University, and Zohar Karti of the Women's Bureau of the Israeli Ministry of Labor; in Austria, Relly Langer of the United States Embassy in Vienna, Senator Anna Demuth, and Edith Krebs of the Women's Division of the Chamber of Labor; Boris Averyanov of the International Department of the all-Russian trade unions; Margarete Mueller of the Women's Division of the East German trade union federation; Ion Ticarau of the International Division of the Romanian trade union federation; in the Federal Republic of Germany, Drs. V. Riefenstahl and L. Joppe of the Federal Institute on Labor (Berlin and Nuremberg respectively), Maria Weber and her assistant I. Blaettel in the German trade union federation together with a host of knowledgeable and helpful women in city federations and in national union headquarters, Dr. Kosmali of the Social Welfare Ministry, and Ms. Glaser of the Women's National Council. The list could be extended a great deal, for everyone who was interviewed expressed interest and was helpful far beyond the call of duty.

I want to add that the presentation and interpretation of the impressions and data collected are entirely my responsibility. For failures to understand or to assimilate information about the countries I visited, I accept full responsibility. For the enrichment of my personal experience and knowledge, I cannot be sufficiently grateful.

Alice H. Cook

INTRODUCTION

For fifteen months in 1972 and 1973 I observed the special problems of working mothers in nine countries — Sweden, Israel, East Germany, West Germany, Romania, Austria, Russia, Japan, and Australia. The experience of country after country discloses how universal are the problems of working mothers.

The deserted, immigrant Australian mother who night after night took her little girl by the hand and walked through her suburb of Sydney knocking on doors to inquire whether anyone was available to care for her child; the Austrian textile workers who regard the hour's ride to work on the company bus as their chief recreation; the Japanese bank teller who brought her six-week-old infant to an unregistered day care center where the baby was swaddled and placed with four others on a shelf running the length of a tiny room, because no public facility was available for children under ten months of age; the Israeli mother whose husband was exhausting himself with three jobs in an attempt to keep up with high costs of living but who herself had to refuse one because there were no after-school care facilities for her two children who finished school at 1:30—all these women were at their wits' ends. They were victims of social circumstance, left unaided to deal with problems so complex and overwhelming they could not identify them all, much less surmount them.

National Differences

Yet basic differences in approach to these problems exist from country to country. The most fundamental perhaps is the difference between communist and noncommunist countries. In the former, it is accepted that women should and will work and that if they are to work at maximum efficiency they will need help with arrangements for child care and for assistance with housework. But even among the communist countries wide variations exist. Some of the differences derive, for example, from population policy, and whether it is to be encouraged or controlled. Some have their roots in decisions about capital investment in consumers' goods and particularly in household appliances (as opposed to the Leninist demand for "industrialization of household work") and find expression, for example, in a decision to build large laundry enterprises rather than family-size washing machines. Some are related to the planners' decision to bring women into the work force and the importance attached therefore to providing child care for infants under two or three years of age, as well as education and skill training for the women themselves, perhaps stingily at the women's own time and expense, perhaps generously stimulated by the offer of released time from work, special recognition, or an increment in pay on completion of the program.

A commitment to equality is common to both communist and noncommunist countries but it is mainly and foremost in Scandinavia that the consequences of this commitment have been incorporated in educational and tax policy, and social programs and welfare facilities have been constructed so as to implement the commitment. Other European countries have studied the Scandinavian model, and the Federal Republic of Germany discusses adapting some of these programs to its own family and social welfare legislation.

On the whole, however, the great distinction between what are popularly called "East" and "West," communist and noncommunist, approaches to the problems of working women is a sharp one. The distinction is one of policies and of the values that are marshaled to explain and justify them. In the West in the name of freedom and individual choice — matters of high valence — individual women who "wish to go to work" are left to solve all the problems of finding jobs, providing child care, and maintaining the home at an acceptable standard on their own. To be sure some of these countries have programs of training and counseling addressed to these women; some provide child care facilities at least to certain categories; some voluntary agencies try to respond to their needs in localities where they can get funding for experiments. By and large, however, national policies overlook the many special and serious problems of these women.

The communist countries, on the other hand, in the name of equal rights and duties to work, and needing the labor of every citizen if industrialization is to go forward rapidly, tend to see the problem of working mothers as calling for social response. Again the programs they provide are often inadequate, though not quite at the level of inadequacy prevailing in the Western world. Provisions for assistance are of course linked to overall social policy including planning of the labor market, in which women are still, despite the rhetoric, often a secondary or supplementary labor force in a system that first draws on the male labor pool and only with its exhaustion or when it is deficient looks to inducing women to enter and remain in the labor force.

The cost of "equality" for women, considering their special problems, is extraordinarily high, as Sweden has carefully calculated. Sweden and the other Scandinavian countries have nevertheless accepted these costs, partly out of national commitment to "equality" and partly because they are convinced that over the middle haul the investment in women's training and support programs will pay for itself and make economic returns to the nation.

Women's Special Needs

I shall argue in this monograph that women in the work force have very special needs that cannot be met merely through slogans of "equality" or piecemeal attempts to introduce equal pay or equal opportunity. These needs are so general as to constitute social problems calling for social solutions.

Basically these needs arise from two factors: the first, the function of women to bear children in their young adulthood, is unchangeable, and the other, the differentiated role assignments given women in the home, in the community, and in the work place, is unchanging. These latter derive, of course, from traditions, biases, and a considerable social history of unequal and often inequitable treatment of women; they have become embedded in law; they find their expression in a division of labor and responsibility in the family. Because family, school, and society generally have imprinted the inevitability of these role differentiations upon both men and women, women themselves by and large accept them. Many of them feel deeply that the weight of their burdens is unfair and unjust, but they have neither the individual strength nor the support of the social institutions that are necessary for change. Yet, so long as society makes these assignments and women accept them as given, they are severely handicapped in their economic functioning.

I hasten to say that I fully recognize that men are as imprisoned in their sex roles as women. Unquestionably many of them envy women their ability to "choose" whether or not and when they will work and would welcome such a possibility for themselves. Undoubtedly work in the menial and repetitive jobs is no more fulfilling for them than it is for women. The fact that work means so much for men and results in their "commitment" to it is as much, of course, a product of their social fate in being assigned to work all their adult lives as women's presumed lack of "commitment" is a product of their chief responsibility for child and family welfare. If men were to have a choice about working, it is altogether probable that they too would want to quit when work is unsatisfactory or when family needs become demands.

The special point about women's work lives, however, is that in both communist and noncommunist countries we have developed only one pattern of work and that is the one which the male can fulfill and to which he has become socialized — the uninterrupted work life beginning at the end of schooling and ending with compulsory retirement. It is structured for the most part to fill eight hours a day, five or six days a week, and forty-eight to fifty-two weeks a year. Sometimes work is scheduled on shifts, occasionally it is seasonal, but the model demands that it be continuous.

If women are to continue to bear children (and who else can do it?) they cannot conform to this model. If children are to be nurtured and cared for by parents for a given period — the period of breast-feeding, or the period of infancy, whether defined as the first six months or the first three years — the mother or the father must be able to remain away from work and with the child during that time. Most societies see no alternative here to the mother doing this. If parents have more than one child, the period of time involved runs not simply to two or three but up to ten years or more. Experience so far, even in the Scandinavian countries where parental equality in this regard has become law, that is, either father or mother may take child care leave without loss of job and for a time without serious loss of income, suggests that these nurturing duties fall almost invariably to the mother. Only a very few experiments suggest the workability of a genuine "exchange of role" model. Certainly no one will dispute that change in this regard may well be the last to take place, so deeply rooted in all value systems is the mother-child relationship.

Thus, given the special functions and needs of women, special work-force and welfare adaptations are necessary. It was these adaptations I was looking for on my travels and it is the practical programs which have evolved from them that I shall treat in this and following monographs.

It is clear now that women and especially mothers are in the work force to stay. Not only are they pushing into the labor market for all the reasons that I shall outline, but the growing service sector in all the modern economies exerts a demand pull on their employment. They will not disappear en masse as they did at the ends of World Wars I and II when men returned and claimed "their jobs." Still, the degree to which societies regard women as a "reserve army" in the labor force is significantly represented in the excessive unemployment of women in the current worldwide depression. The problem is not one that can be patched up or swept under the rug or put off for a better day. It is large, rapidly growing, insistent, and socially significant.

In considering the problems that working mothers around the world have to deal with, I shall limit myself to matters that are of concern in all the social systems I looked at. Even then the list is long. In enumerating it, I run the risk of repeating views and facts put forward by other writers. What I am trying to do here is to focus on two aspects of women's current concerns, on *mothers* and on *work,* and it is that particular territory that I want to map out in sufficient detail.

Because communist and noncommunist definitions of the problems differ and approaches vary, I shall briefly outline ways in which both kinds of societies are addressing these matters, as I treat them one by one.

In the concluding section of this monograph I will outline at least one approach that can be taken not only to relieve women of their heaviest burdens but to release their economic potential for themselves and for society.

I. Numbers

The number of mothers who work is growing. Married women represent the largest single additional increment to the work force over the past five to ten years and are, thus, the outstanding element of structural change in the labor market.

The number of working mothers is growing in nearly every country. Table 1 includes most of the countries covered in this study and shows not only the extent of female participation, but also the high percentage of married women, in the labor force.[1]

In recent years, the proportion of married women among female employees has risen rapidly. In Japan, for example, the movement looked like this:

Year	Percentage of married women among all Japanese female employees
1955	20.9
1966	35.9
1970	41.4
1972	46.1
1974	50.6

The increase of paid female employees[2] in Japan between 1960 and 1970 was 4 million, of whom well over half were married.

In Australia, female participation in the labor force shows a steady increase since the end of the World War II. From 1971 to 1974, it rose from 39.4 percent to 41.4 percent of all women of working age. In the same period men's participation declined by 0.9 percent and single females' by 2.6 percent. The participation rate of married women, however, increased by 4.2 percentage points, from 35.2 percent to 39.4 percent.

The number of mothers working in West Germany almost doubled between 1950 and 1970, with the result that by 1970 when 46.2 percent of all

---

1. Since most statisticians develop labor-force participation rates for married women rather than mothers and since most married women have children, I am using the statistics for working married women as roughly equivalent to working mothers.

2. Employees are defined as persons who work for wages or profit for unincorporated enterprises, companies, corporations, or associations, and government. For married women as a percentage of the female labor force, see table 1.

Table 1: Women in the Labor Force: Selected Countries

Country	Date	Working women		Married women in the labor force	
		Percent of women age 15 and over	Percent of labor force	Percent of all married women	Percent of female labor force
Australia	1974	41.4	33.9	39.4	63.7
Austria	1973			44.1	58.4
	1975	44.0[a]	36.5		
Canada	1974	39.7[b]	34.4	36.7	57.1
Denmark	1970	33.0	36.5	45.6[c]	59.2
Finland	1970	36.8	42.2	55.6[c]	59.9
Germany, East	1975	55.7[d]	49.6[d]		
Germany, West	1974	38.9	36.8	35.9	60.1
Great Britain	1971	42.7	37.8	42.2	62.1
Israel	1972	30.8[b]	31.1	24.0	57.7
Japan	1974	46.6	37.8	45.8	62.6
Norway[e]	1975	41.0[f]	37.4	44.3	66.2
Sweden[g]	1974	48.0[f]	38.5	46.0	58.9
United States	1975	45.9[h]	39.5	44.4	57.8
USSR	1974	86.0[i]	51.0		

NOTE: The labor force comprises employed persons, including unpaid family workers, and unemployed persons.

a. Age 15–65.
b. Age 14 and over.
c. Employed married women *with children* as a percentage of all married women.
d. Women age 15–60, men age 15–65.
e. Data are for employed persons only.
f. Age 16–74.
g. Data are for employed persons working at least twenty hours a week.
h. Age 16 and over.
i. Ages uncertain.

SOURCES: The data for Australia, Austria, East Germany, West Germany, Israel, and Norway are from the statistical yearbooks of these countries; the *Yearbook of Nordic Statistics* provided the data for Denmark and Finland. Other sources include *Women in the Labour Force: Facts and Figures* from the Women's Bureau of Labour Canada; *The Role and Status of Women Workers in the U.S. and Japan,* published by the Women's and Minors' Bureau of the Japanese Ministry of Labor; *Women and Work: A Statistical Survey,* published by the British Department of Employment; *Fact Sheets on Sweden;* and S. Turchaninova, "Trends in Women's Employment in the USSR." U.S. data are from H. Hayghe, "Marital and Family Characteristics of the Labor Force, March 1975."

women between the ages of 15 and 65 were working, 39.1 percent of all married women, 35.7 percent of all mothers with children, and 43 percent of all widowed and divorced women were working.

In Sweden between 1965 and 1975 the proportion of women between 16 and 74 years of age who were working and the proportion of those working who had young children both increased markedly:

Year	Percentage of all Swedish women between ages 16 and 74 working	Percentage of all women in Swedish labor force with children under 7
1965	48.7	
1968		42.1
1972	54.7	53.7
1975	59.2	60.5

The percentage of all married women in Sweden who were gainfully employed and working at least half time rose from 9 percent in 1930 to 15.6 percent in 1950; by 1970 it had reached 44.9 percent and in 1974 stood at 46 percent.

In Austria the participation of women in the work force has been comparatively high until recent years when it fell from its fifty-year level of about 40 percent to its present 36.5 percent. The proportion of married women working, however, has been steadily rising. In 1961 married women made up about 45 percent of the female work force; in 1971, 56.2 percent; and in 1973, 58.4 percent. The proportion of these with children of school age rose from about 50 percent in 1961 to 54.7 percent in 1969. Later census data are not available at this writing.

In the communist countries the constitutions prescribe both the right and duty of all women to work, and the expectations of women themselves are that they will work with only brief interruptions for childbearing. All communist countries show a high labor-force participation of women, including married women and mothers.

The Russian census of 1959 suggested there was a large pool of women employed only in households, but between then and the census of 1970, Feshbach and Rapawy report, "the number of persons in able-bodied ages who were employed only in households dropped from 17.9 to 5.9 million persons."[3] Of this latter figure at least 4.5 million are women "of whom two-thirds have children under 16 years of age, are relatively poorly qualified or have never worked and of whom only 9% had higher education and 45% had only elementary education." Some 10 million women, according to these same authors, were brought into production between 1961 and 1967 and "by 1970, this reservoir was being depleted." Lapidus in dealing with figures for 1972 essentially confirms this trend and reports that "close to 85 percent of all

3. This monograph has been written to avoid the use of footnotes except where definitions seem necessary. Full citations for books and authors referred to in the text may be found in the bibliography.

Soviet women between the ages of 20 and 55 are currently employed outside the home."

In East Germany, perhaps as many as 80 percent of all women of working age, married and unmarried, are employed.[4] In the less developed communist economies the percentage is not so high—Berent shows that in Czechoslovakia in 1961 53.4 percent of all women 15 years of age and over, and 55.1 percent of all married women 15 years of age and over, were working. For Hungary in 1960 it was 43.4 percent of all women 15 years of age and over. As in Russia, however, development will call forth a higher percentage of the able-bodied wives and mothers from their families and put them to work in the productive economy.

---

4. In 1964 Berent put this figure at 70 percent of all women aged 18–49 and 64.8 percent of all married women in that age group, while he showed that 83 percent of women with no children worked and 77.3 percent of all married women with no children worked.

II. Why Women Work

Mothers work for economic reasons: many be-
cause they are single, divorced, separated, or
deserted and thus heads of families; others be-
cause their husbands are incapacitated, unskil-
led, unemployed, or simply earn too little to sup-
port families on a single income. Mothers also
work because they come to need a life outside the
home as well as inside it, if they are to maintain
emotional health.

The reasons women work are not hard to find. Demographic changes in the postwar years are a major factor. The birthrate in most industrial countries has fallen sharply and fairly continuously since World War II. In the countries covered in this study women are generally having fewer than three children. In Sweden half the families have only one child. Marriages tend to occur at younger ages, and, where this is the case, women are through with childbearing and often with early child care by the time they are thirty. The coresident family is rarely extended to a third generation or to in-laws and cousins; it is a nuclear group of parents and one, two, or at most three children. More and more frequently the family is headed by a single parent. The increase in divorce, separation, and desertion has greatly enlarged the number of women who are heads of families and as such the sole or major breadwinners. In the Scandinavian countries, and particularly Sweden, a sharp rise in the number of single parents has followed a gradual change in the values attached to marriage. Indeed, 25 percent of the children born in 1972 were to nonmarried parents, and in many cases the mother and her child constituted the family.

A commonly held view in Western countries is that women should and do have a choice as to whether they will work or stay at home. This view is often put forward as a circumstance in marked contrast to the case of women in communist countries, who, it is pointed out, are "forced" to go to work. The fact seems to be that millions of women whether they live in Russia or elsewhere have no choice but to work.

In every country, the number of women who work because they must earn a living is very high. Some are heads of families; some are wives of men who are unemployed or ill or incapacitated; some support parents or other family members. In many families in both the East and the West the wages of a single breadwinner, male or female, are inadequate to maintain an acceptable standard of health and decency. Whether as a measure of low productivity or as part of a design to compel women as well as men to work, wages in the communist countries are set so low as to act as one of several forces bringing women into employment. Moreover, the rising level of consumer wants means that a single income rarely suffices to meet wishes for comfort, leisure, and education, while worldwide inflation severely aggravates these pressures on family income.

But women do not work for economic reasons alone. Most workers, whether men or women, find their jobs are drudging, repetitious, hard, noisy, even grimy; they have few choices in their work, little participation in making decisions, and little self-direction. Jobs leave very little room for anything that can be called "fulfillment," despite the fact that the women's liberation movement in its campaign for equal opportunity for women tends to see work as a necessary element in women's "self-actualization." And yet, in the sense that jobs make women part of a social group — enabling women to have human adult contacts with fellow workers, and to earn money that they can to some extent control — they represent some measure of "fulfillment," and as such they are as important to women as to men. Women in factories frequently volunteered how much they "enjoyed" work, because they were "with such a nice group of mates" or "out of the house" or "able to do so much better with the kids because I don't have to be with them all day."

Whether the causes bringing women to work are demographic, psychological, educational, or economic, they suggest that working mothers are a permanent addition to the labor force. During World War II women poured into the male world of work because the men had left to fight the war; when the men returned the women went home or were sent home. On one day in 1946 in Japan, 11,000 women were dismissed by the Japan National Railways alone. The jobs then presumably belonged to the men and men reclaimed them. But the reasons mothers work in the 1970s cannot be found in a single cause or a momentary historical crisis. They are long-range and probably irreversible. Women are in the labor market to stay.

III. Women Are Different

Women's work lives proceed at a different rhythm from men's. They are marked by interruptions for pregnancy, maternity, and child care. In a world of work fashioned and fitted to men, these interruptions handicap women in finding jobs, receiving training, and being considered for promotion, that is, for the rewards presumably attractive in economic life.

Norms of work life have developed to fit the uninterrupted — the male — career. Women cannot match this pattern, because they interrupt work life to bear children and to care for them. For the most part in the Western industrial world there has been little recognition in the labor market of women's life pattern. Or, to put it more accurately, there has been little effort to accommodate work life to it. Historically, housework and child care took so high a proportion of women's lives that there was little time left for gainful employment. In the mid-1970s, the actual years devoted to childbearing and childrearing are few. Adult life, following this stage, has lengthened dramatically, even more for women than for men. When women return to work after maternal interruption, they have a long period, maybe twenty to thirty years, ahead of them during which most of them will continue to work.

American experience in this regard is more striking than other countries, though to some degree they are all approaching the same figures. According to the Women's Bureau of the United States Department of Labor in 1975, 61 percent of the women 20–24 years of age are workers — this corresponds to premarriage and early marriage years. The figure drops to 51.8 percent between the ages of 25–34 as children are born and come to school age. It rises again to 54.6 percent in the 35–44 age group and to 54.9 percent in the 45–54 age bracket. The percentage of women 55–64 who work is 41.7 percent. The median age of the American working woman is 36. This recession and accession in the proportion of women working in middle age has been described as an "M" graph. (In the 1960 census the proportion of women of 55–64 who were working equaled that of the 25–34 age bracket.) It has, however, as we can see, become less accentuated both in its decline and rise and now indicates that fewer women leave the labor force than formerly did. Of those who leave, fewer remain out for long periods, and those who return remain for at least twenty years.

The Women's Bureau further notes:

The recent rise in the labor force participation rate of young women in their twenties and early thirties has been most striking among mothers. For example, while the labor force participation rate of all women 20 to 24 rose from 45 percent in 1960 to 61 percent in 1974, the rate for wives in this age group with children under 6 doubled from 18 to 37 percent.

The degree to which other countries approach or duplicate this pattern varies, with regard to the point of retirement from the labor force and of reentry, but the rising proportion of married women and mothers working clearly points to the fact that working women either remain in the labor force with only minor interruptions or return after shorter periods of interruption.

The West Germans and Japanese report that a higher percentage of young women return to work soon after childbirth but quit work when the children are ready for kindergarten and schools. At this time traditional demands on the middle-class mother to supplement formal schooling with supervision of homework and provision of extracurricular learning, such as music, travel, and reading, increase markedly. The return to work in those countries accordingly tends to involve women in their late thirties and early to mid-forties.

Table 2: Women's Labor-force Participation Rates by Age Group (In Percent)

Country	Year	15–19	20–24	25–29	30–34	35–39	40–44	45–49	50–54
Austria	1971	60.0	68.0	56.2		51.6		53.7	48.5
Australia	1971	52.1	58.6	39.1		42.4		43.1	36.4
Canada	1971	37.0	62.8	47.2		43.0		45.4	43.3
Finland	1975	30.9	66.5	75.5		81.0		73.8	
Germany, East	1971		74.6	79.3	79.6			79.8	73.6
Germany, West	1975	50.7	68.4	56.7		50.8		51.6	47.4
Great Britain	1971	55.7	60.1	43.0		53.0		61.5	58.6
Israel	1974		41.4ᵃ		40.5		37.3		35.7
Japan	1975	22.6	66.6	43.5		51.3		62.2	58.6
Romania	1966	50.8	74.3	78.5		78.4		75.2	71.3
Sweden	1970	52.2ᵇ	71.1	70.3		73.8		77.9	71.2
United States	1975	49.0ᵇ	64.0	56.9		54.0		55.6	53.0
USSR	1970			86.3		92.7		90.6	77.3

a. 18–24.
b. 16–19.
SOURCE: International Labour Organisation, *Yearbook of Labour Statistics, 1976.*

The figures in table 2 demonstrate a critical matter. The interruption in women's careers occurs at a time when men are getting started in their careers and being looked over as likely candidates for advanced training in skills and for supervision. When women return to work they are above the age limit that employers usually consider sound for such investment. (Years ago in his study *The Auto Worker and the American Dream,* Eli Chinoy pointed out that the man-on-the-line who has not become a foreman by age thirty-two will never make it.)

IV. Women's Jobs

Working mothers, even more than working women, generally are restricted to a narrow list of occupations, which are characterized by low skill, low rates of pay, and low income.

When women are ready to go to work, whether it is a first attempt to locate work or reentry after considerable absence, the work they find is in the narrow range of typical women's occupations. They work on assembly lines in electronic factories and operate textile and sewing machines. They serve as clerks, typists, and receptionists in offices; as nurses and paraprofessionals in health and child care institutions; as waitresses, maids, and cooks in hospitals, hotels, and restaurants. They are saleswomen in retail stores and cashiers at checkout counters in supermarkets. If they have college degrees, they teach school, work as librarians and social workers or, in the business world, as assistant personnel directors, girls Friday, and public relations aides. All these typically women's jobs are low-paid, low-scale, low-key.

Pross found, for example, in the Common Market countries that three-quarters of the women in her sample whether white- or blue-collar workers were "at the bottom of the hierarchy of work." Three-quarters of the blue-collar women workers were unskilled or semiskilled. "Skilled women workers made up a very modest minority of the total group of women workers," ranging from 3 percent in Italy to 21 percent in Belgium. The Federal Republic of Germany, Holland, and Luxemburg each showed 13 percent of the sample in that category. "Among the white-collar workers, inferior positions dominate." A study by the Munich Institute for Social Science Research in 1969 found that 60 percent of all employed women earned less than 600 marks per month net, and in 1970 the average gross earnings of women in industry were 31 percent lower than those of men.

Similar evidence mounts in every country. Again we turn to comparative statistics to see that in all the countries investigated women cluster in clerical, sales, and service work and have a distinct minority status in the crafts and in executive and administrative posts (table 3).

Nowhere, not even in the USSR, are women distributed throughout the range of occupations. In the communist countries, as in the West, women tend to be clustered in the typical women's jobs — in textiles and electronics, in the blue-collar occupations, in lower level white-collar and service jobs, in nursing, and in primary school teaching.

Berent reports that the participation of women in textiles, for example, is 78 percent in Bulgaria, 70 percent in East Germany, 68 percent in Hungary, 64 percent in Poland, and 74 percent in the USSR. The food processing industry records 60 percent of its employees as female in Bulgaria, 51 percent in East Germany, 45 percent in Hungary, and 55 percent in the USSR. Although

Table 3: Percentage of Women in Total Labor Force
in Seven Occupational Groups

Country	Year	Professional, technical, and related workers	Administrative, executive, and managerial workers	Clerical workers	Sales workers	Craftsmen and production workers	Service workers	Farmers and fishermen
Austria	1975		43.7[a]		56.7	16.9	68.7	48.2
Australia	1971	42.3	12.0	63.8	48.3	13.4	62.7	15.5
Canada	1976	48.2	20.2	74.6	34.5	12.2	50.5	18.6
Finland	1975	45.0	17.9	82.3	55.3	24.3	83.8	44.9
Germany, West	1970	34.3	13.5	54.6	52.7	17.3	54.6	48.1
Israel	1975	50.3	7.4	55.4	28.6	10.8	52.3	20.1
Japan	1975	38.4	5.3	49.6	39.3	24.0	53.5	49.3
Romania	1966	44.4	40.5		40.7	17.7	48.6	58.6
Sweden	1975	48.1	11.3	78.4	47.6	17.4	78.0	24.3
United Kingdom	1971	38.3	8.4	60.3	47.4	17.1	69.3	13.1
United States	1975	41.6	19.7	78.1	43.5	17.9	62.3	15.9

a. Combined percentage for the first three occupational groups.
Source: International Labour Organisation, *Yearbook of Labour Statistics*, 1976.

women have unquestionably entered the engineering trades in greater numbers in the communist countries than elsewhere, they still make up only 25
percent in Bulgaria, 22 percent in East Germany, 33 percent in Hungary, 18
percent in Poland, and 40 percent in the USSR.

Women are predominant in the medical profession in Russia and the
other eastern communist countries, but there wages for doctors are set slightly
below those for highly skilled blue-collar workers (110 rubles as compared with
120), and very few women indeed are surgeons or heads of clinics and
hospitals.

The degree to which women are represented in various occupations in the
United States, as table 3 shows, is not essentially different from that of the
other countries. Moreover, as shown in table 4, segregation of women in the
so-called female occupations has either actually increased or shown little
change over the twenty-seven-year period from 1950 to 1977.

Table 4: Major Occupational Groups of Employed Women in
the United States: 1950, 1968, 1977[a]

Major occupational group	Percent distribution			As percent of total employed by occupation		
	1950	1968	1977	1950	1968	1977
Total	100.0	100.0	100.0	29.3[b]	36.6[b]	40.7[b]
Professional and technical workers	10.8	14.4	16.1	41.8	38.6	42.7
Managers, officials, proprietors (non-farm)	5.5	4.3	5.7	14.8	15.7	22.3
Clerical workers	26.4	33.3	35.1	59.3	72.6	79.4
Sales workers	8.8	6.8	6.7	39.0	39.7	48.2
Craftsmen, foremen	1.1	1.1	1.6	2.4	3.3	5.1
Operatives	18.7	14.8	11.8	26.9	29.9	42.1
Non-farm laborers	.4	.4	1.1	2.2	3.5	9.4
Private household workers	10.3	7.2	3.0	92.1	97.6	97.4
Service workers (except private household)	12.6	15.6	17.8	45.4	57.0	57.9
Farmers, farm managers	1.5	.3	.3	5.5	4.1	6.3
Farm laborers, foremen	3.9	1.7	1.0	27.4	28.0	27.4

a. Data, based on women 14 years of age and over in 1950 and 1968, and 16 years of age and
over in 1977, are for April of each year.
b. Total employed women as a percentage of all employed persons.

Sources: Based on table 40 from *Handbook on Women Workers*, U.S. Women's Bureau
Bulletin 294 (Washington, D.C.: GPO, 1969), p. 92; and U.S. Department of Labor, Bureau of
Labor Statistics, *Employment and Earnings* (May 1977), table A-21.

The reasons are not far to seek. Women's education is apt to be less than men's. Pross found this so in all the Common Market countries. Vocational training is less available to them and, where it is open, it too is restricted to the women's trades. Hardly a country exists in which hairdressing is not the major apprenticed trade for girls. Interruption of work by itself is a deterrent to women's access to jobs on reentry into the labor market. When women interrupt work even for only a few years, they become to some degree estranged from work, they lose some skill, and they inevitably fail to keep abreast of changing technology and process. The woman who has been away from work for several years may on return find that her old job has vanished into the computer; at the very least her manually operated typewriter is now electrical. The assembly of television sets or toasters or frypans includes new elements that have to be put in place with new tools. New drugs are in the hospital cabinets; new teaching machines in the school learning centers. Her dexterity with the soldering iron, the ampule, the business machine, or the tape recorder has deteriorated. Labor law, labor relations, pay scales, bonus systems, deducts have all changed. It's a different world from the one she left.

Women's opportunities for getting job information, counseling, refresher courses, or training are very few and only unsystematically available. Small wonder that women turn to jobs that are close to home, where their neighbors work, where little is demanded. Once in such jobs the chances for growth, training, and promotion are small indeed. Employers think of training, when they think of it for women at all, in terms of younger, single, or at least childless women — women who will as nearly as possible accept for themselves the norms associated with men's uninterrupted work lives.

Some exceptions to these generalizations are beginning to be visible. Employers in Japan, in Austria, and in Australia, for example, where the labor market is extremely tight, have begun to recruit older women. Where this is going on the public employment offices in a few instances have been available to help find these women and to set up short programs that will give older women some idea of what the labor market may be for them. In Vienna, Austria, the purpose of such a "course," which has about a week's duration, is to acquaint these women with work managers, who talk to them about jobs they can do, and with work places, which they visit. When women indicate some interest in finding work, they can get counseling on training and placement. A high percentage of the women attending these programs actually find permanent jobs. But, as useful as these programs are in encouraging women to return to work, they do nothing to widen the range of jobs available to women. The training they provide is no more than short refresher courses. Their main function is not to improve women's working conditions but to bring to the labor force women who might otherwise never gather the self-confidence to come to an employment office.

Some countries, however, are adjusting their manpower and training programs to the fact of women's reentry into the labor market. They are recognizing that large numbers now do return to work, some of them even while they are still in their early or middle thirties. Some have married so young that they worked only briefly before becoming full-time housewives and mothers. Some have only worked as casuals and now wish to make up for schooling or training they never had. Some wish to make a completely new start, having learned in maturity that the teen-age vocational choices were not

the best. Sweden, Australia, Israel, and Germany, as well as Austria, have
introduced programs designed to meet these needs. Of these, however, only
Sweden, as we shall see, has included in its planning any element that might
bring women in substantial numbers even over the long run into a wider range
of occupations including some of the skilled trades where better pay and
greater opportunity would be accessible.

A brief description of some of these programs will show both what they are
doing and what they are not doing to affect the range, the status, and the
distribution of women's jobs.

The West German Institute of Labor (Bundesanstalt fuer Arbeit) adminis-
ters the country's unemployment funds and with them supports training designed to respond to labor market needs. Although a special section designs
programs for women reentering the labor force, it falls short of achieving its
purpose. Like men, women are offered the inducement of generous credit for
earlier work experience (including the work of housewifery) so as to shorten
the relatively long training periods that German skills normally require.
Moreover enrollees in the program earn something like 80 percent of wages
while they are in training. Nevertheless, women's response to the program is
disappointing. An institute representative with whom I talked attributed this
deficiency to several factors peculiar to women's circumstances. They are
often not free to go where courses are given; they cannot devote full time to
training, even when they are not yet at work; nor can they readily move from
one labor market to another where jobs may be open. Many of them, once they
have decided to go to work, cannot or will not take the time for training. The
institute has therefore provided a second scheme under which employers are
induced to offer on-the-job training to women. Under it, women receive a full
wage from the beginning of employment, and the employer gets a subsidy to
make up the difference between real earnings and pay. This subsidy gradually
diminishes over a scheduled period during which the woman acquires skill and
speed, until she is earning her full wage.

Israel, too, has a number of training programs for mature women, a
substantial number of which are directed more toward orientation and retraining of immigrants than toward the problem of reentry as such. They are,
however, without exception, whether under public or voluntary agency
sponsorship, limited to the "women's trades" — mainly sewing, hotel and
restaurant work, and hairdressing, with a few classes in leather manufacture
and elementary industrial drafting.

Australia's Ministry of Labour in recent years has offered a program called
"Employment Training Scheme for Women." Designed to offer preparatory or
refresher training that will enable women to take up paid employment, the
program is open to both married and adult single women who have "withdrawn
from employment because of domestic responsibilities." These are defined to
include women engaged in unpaid home duties involving care of children or
husband or parent or relative, and the program is meant to be available to
widows, divorcees, single mothers, deserted wives, and women whose husbands are in mental institutions. The training to qualify must be of a type that
can lead to available employment immediately. While academic training is not
excluded, nursing is outside the program since the nursing schools themselves encourage this group of women to take training. The scheme provides
training for a period of up to twelve months full time or two years part time,

although women are officially discouraged from taking the part-time program. Study may be undertaken in residence or by correspondence. The ministry offers payment of all fees for tuition, examinations, and certificates; an incidental weekly expense allowance; travel fares; a living-away-from-home allowance if the training is not available in the hometown; a book allowance; and, for women eligible for unemployment benefits, a maintenance allowance that roughly corresponds to the benefit. The scheme also includes, when the employer agrees to participate, the possibility of in-plant training whereby the employer receives a subsidy of a diminishing percentage of the award wage while the worker is paid in full.

Australia's success rate is considerably higher than Germany's in terms of attracting and holding women candidates for training. The program is fully subscribed. Of the persons accepted for training 69 percent were completing training in 1973. Most of the candidates go into office work and three-quarters of the applicants go to business colleges or into the business departments of the local technical colleges. The Melbourne officer in charge of the Victoria program said that a high percentage of these women get jobs on completion of the program and that older women had better records of placement than younger ones but the percentage of placement for all occupations and ages was 90 percent.

It is clear here as elsewhere that the purpose of these programs is directed more to getting women back into the labor market than to increasing their range of jobs. They are unquestionably helpful in lifting the level both of their enrollees' self-confidence and of their skill. They are not aimed at breaking the occupational barriers or lifting the low ceilings that confine women's jobs in their present narrow limits.

Whereas these countries rarely use their training schemes to broaden the narrow range of women's occupations, Swedish employment officers (known as "activators") are constantly working with employers and with women applicants to break down the traditional occupational and skill barriers.

Sweden has perhaps the most carefully worked out scheme for training and retraining married women who are ready to enter the labor force. When these married women report at the employment exchange, they are immediately eligible for vocational counseling and labor market training programs, covering a wide range of occupations. Moreover, they are eligible for supportive aid, including payments to cover child care, transportation, school fees and tuition, and textbooks. Sweden's Labor Market Board is ready to finance long-range as well as short-range training and sends many adults to residence programs for a year or more in the Folk High Schools or permits them to make up general education. Forty-three percent of those enrolled in these programs are women. I visited a kraft paper mill in Sweden where no women had previously held production jobs but whose management had agreed to take all women who would complete a three-month training program. Of thirty enrollees, twenty-seven had finished and all of these had been placed in integrated work groups throughout the plant. A year and a half later when I was there, all twenty-seven were still employed.

Sweden, moreover, is ready to go to the very roots of sex inequality and so to begin to lift the double burden that working women everywhere carry for home and children as well as work. This aspect of the problem is considered in more detail in the section on child care and other homemaking services.

The communist countries by contrast do not have to deal to any great extent with women taking long leave from the labor force. Women are encouraged to work with only short breaks of perhaps three months at childbirth and most of the countries have made heavy investments in child care facilities, including facilities for infants, so that the mother is available for work. In Romania, I heard repeatedly about the measures that permit women to take unpaid leave for as long as six years to be with their children before they start to school. Repeated inquiries in the many plants I visited failed to produce evidence that women do so or indeed that women are very generally aware of the possibility.

The problems that many of these countries have had to cope with are women's very poor general education; the heavy weight of tradition, which continues to draw women in large numbers to the classic women's occupations; and the failure of girls to avail themselves of vocational training, particularly in the technical and scientific occupations. Moreover, many women, and especially those with large families and those living outside the industrial centers, have been unable to find suitable child care facilities and therefore remain at home until well into middle age. It is precisely these older women who finished school at a point when no more than seven or eight years of elementary education were required and before the present lengthened and improved education was available to them. Just as much as their sisters in the West, these women suffer the inferiority of their preparation for the more remunerative jobs in modern industry.

In East Germany where the need for women workers is more pressing even than it is in Russia, a great deal of emphasis in recent years has been put on on-the-job training for mature women, partly to enhance their efficiency, partly to provide the basis for more specialized and advanced training. While presumably all training programs are open to women on the same terms as they are to men, special courses have everywhere been organized for women alone. Such programs are part of the factory plan and as such are subject to requirements and rewards for fulfillment as rigorous as those for production itself. Each factory must report the number of women it will train each year, the precise jobs for which they are being trained, and the plans worked out for selecting and schooling them. Training is divided into component building blocks that can be added end to end to constitute journeyman's, master's, and foreman's training. Women completing each block of the total program automatically receive higher pay as well as intangible rewards of recognition.

A reassessment of the problem of reentry is overdue. The customary and unthinking approach to women workers in most industrial countries is to assume that the uninterrupted career is not only normative but necessary. Women who cannot do all that men do, and in addition take care of children *and* get supper on the table, are somehow deficient. If they cannot make up for time and training lost during their absence from the labor market, they must be content, so folk wisdom goes, with unskilled, low-paid jobs. That's all they're able to take on.

Is it not possible, however, even under the freewheeling, unregimented, individualistic values of the West, to begin to accept and deal with the fact that mature women, usually mothers of children, will be entering or reentering the labor market at a point where most training opportunities are closed to them?

To do so, would of course mean recognition of the specific female work pattern, which involves interruption and reentry, even late decisions about occupations and careers. Some of the possibilities include vocational counseling for adults tied into the employment offices, public school vocational programs, or technical colleges and reappraisal by employers of the probable payoff for investments in on-the-job and released-time training opportunities for these women. Perhaps most significant would be for educational institutions — community colleges, adult education programs, and the four-year institutions — to plan their offerings to meet these women's needs not only in regard to courses but to schedules allowing for part-time work, daytime classes geared to the hours of kindergartens and child care centers (even the provision of child care facilities during class and study hours), and access to loan and scholarship schemes.

A second kind of reassessment directed to the demands of modern industry on its workers could result in a redefinition of the work ethic and with it of work life for both men and women. Our grandfathers and grandmothers in those "dark satanic mills" in the nineteenth century worked from sunup to sundown, partly because their agrarian counterparts had to do the same, partly because work was insurance against the devil's appropriation of idle hands. Yet, during the first quarter of the twentieth century, the eight-hour day had become accepted as the standard or an immediately desirable goal. In the United States, discussion has moved in recent years to longer annual leaves, to considering lowering the age of retirement for both men and women, providing sabbatic leaves for industrial workers, and instituting four-day weeks. Change in many aspects of scheduling work has resulted in a significant modification of the ways of looking at lifetime work commitment. Is it not possible that such adjustments could result in narrowing the differences between the rhythm of men's and women's work lives, allowing periods of interruption for both sexes? To the degree that happens, opportunities for training would have to be redistributed through adult life, with great advantages for women.

But until such far-reaching changes take place, special attention here and now needs to be directed toward the graph of women's working years and their need for counseling, training, and job openings when they return to work.

V. Women and Education

Women's commitment to work rises with educational level, even when such factors as numbers of children and income are held constant. Nevertheless, the jobs held by educated women frequently underuse their training and capacities.

Women's commitment to work and their performance at work generally rise with education in both the communist and the noncommunist world.[1] Even at levels below college, the more education a woman has had, the more probable it is that she will work. In the United States in 1974 the level of education of employed women was 12.5 years, a figure which is slightly higher than that of the total female population (12.2 years) and exactly equal to that of working men.

A college education produces women with a view of work and career more closely resembling that of men than is the case with women of lesser education. They are more likely than are their less well educated sisters to work throughout their lives, to have very brief interruptions of work for childbearing, and, because they are apt to bear fewer children, they are likely to have fewer interruptions of any length. These women unquestionably are in a better position to cope. They are presumably in the upper brackets of earners and can therefore afford household help or satisfactory private child care institutions. They thus escape both the financial stringencies that put private child care beyond the reach of factory and service workers and the limitation in numbers of places in publicly subsidized institutions. These women also may be presumed to be married to well-educated husbands, husbands who are more apt than the average to be open-minded about sharing household tasks and to accept their wives' commitment to careers.

Moreover, the jobs these women get are on the whole interesting, even challenging, certainly when compared to those available to women in manufacturing, offices, and restaurants. For them, work can take on meaning for its own sake and begin to exert its own dynamic power over the personality of the woman worker, her commitment to a specific job and her ordering of personal priorities.

Three aspects of women's education are of special concern here. One is the degree to which young women in fact get general education of equal

---

1. This correlation is perhaps most striking in Israel, where the Women's Bureau of the Labor Ministry reports that about 85 percent of college-trained women work even when they have as many as four children, while only about 12 percent of uneducated or poorly educated Israeli women work outside the home. In other countries this correlation is somewhat less pronounced, and in Japan it would seem to be reversed. There women with college educations are not particularly sought by employers, who see them as overqualified for women's work and unlikely to remain in employment for more than the few years between college graduation and marriage.

quality with that of young men and are thus prepared to compete on an equal footing in the labor market. Another is women's access to vocational training and apprenticeships. Both these matters have to do with equal opportunity in preparation for work. The third concern is the degree to which the training of women, particularly those who have had higher education, is fully used and wanted.

In many countries, though not in the United States or Japan, women's secondary educational attainments lag behind those of men. The discrepancy sets in at once with the completion of compulsory education. Indeed, in the state of Hesse in West Germany this difference is already apparent at school-leaving. Of the children finishing their ninth year of school in 1968, 52.5 percent were male and 47.5 percent female.

Three-fourths of the Italian women in the Pross sample of blue- and white-collar workers finished their schooling when the period of compulsory education ended. In Belgium it was two-thirds, in Germany half, and in France 70 percent. Pross comments, "It is not too much to assume that this [low grade of education] makes many of them susceptible to manipulation and to the indirect influences of a tradition which disadvantages them." When children are no longer required to go to school, or must pay tuition to go to higher school, it is the girls who drop out in larger numbers than the boys. Moreover where girls' and boys' education is segregated or where special curricula are devised for them separately, girls frequently receive less academic training, are less well prepared for further education, and receive prevocational or vocational training in a very limited number of women's (i.e., low-paid) occupations. A state legislator in Bavaria related one such example. Girls at the high school level there are required to spend so much time on their home economics subjects that general preparation for higher education is slighted to their disadvantage in gaining admission to a university.

Women have less opportunity, because of their home responsibilities, to take advantage of evening schools and other adult education programs, which for persons of middle age may be the one possibility for making up deficient schooling. This disadvantage assumes special importance in countries where the school systems have greatly changed and the years of compulsory education increased within recent years, a circumstance which obtains in nearly all the European countries, communist and noncommunist.

One reason, then, that adult women are assigned to unskilled and low-paid work is that their general educational background tends to be lower than men's. But this is not the whole story. Their in-school and postschool vocational training is either totally lacking or very deficient when compared with men's. Women's access to vocational training is everywhere very limited. According to a government report on vocational training in the progressive province of Hesse, West Germany, "the number of apprenticeships available for girls is very limited, and in industry and handwork is about three times as many for boys as for girls." In a study of girls' education throughout the Federal Republic, Maria Borris found decided differences in the instruction of boys and girls in the natural sciences and in practical handwork (such as sewing and home economics), areas in which the traditional concepts of separate education for girls are still very widely held. "In most of the provinces, a basis is laid in elementary school for sex-role typed activities." For example, "boys are directed to 'creative patterns,' the girls to order, cleanliness, and discipline." As for vocational education, while only 6.7 percent of the boys reject training and become unskilled workers, more than 20.9 percent of the girls are in this category. And in the nonacademic secondary schools,

> the instruction in practical subjects inevitably has a negative influence on the girls' intelligence. Even if one leaves out the possibility that the exclusively oriented instruction [is an intellectual disadvantage], there remains the disorienting effect of the total society's view of division of work.... Only the academic preparatory schools — the gymnasia — provide a preparation for scientific-theoretical orientation in the world of knowledge. (my translation)

Opportunities for women to learn trades in most countries exist only in a limited number of areas; mainly in clerical work, hairdressing, and the textile trades. A report by the Organization for Economic Cooperation and Development (OECD) entitled *Employment of Women* sums up the situation.

> Fewer girls receive vocational training, while the range of courses provided is much more limited. ... Vocational training as at present available for women limits their capacity for employment.

Nor can these lacks be made up once women go back to work. Pross points out that for the western European countries these shortages in women's education are not compensated for in the factories; and indeed "in every country, the significance of the factory as a training center is very slight."

Even in the case of comparatively well educated women, a marked characteristic of their employment is underuse of their education and capacities. In part this occurs because in professional careers, as in the drudging jobs, women carry their double burden. Realization of the demands on them outside of work skews their own choices in the direction of the routine, sedentary, scheduled occupations for a significant number of years. They opt for institutional rather than free employment in the professions, for lectureships rather than professorships at universities. They seek part-time work despite its limitations on progression. They take on helping rather than managerial roles. They eschew jobs that require travel or irregular hours.

Even in the communist countries, these considerations tend to operate. A woman who sits on the executive committee of the party and of the trade unions in the German Democratic Republic discussed with me the difficulty in finding women available for high positions.The problem, she said, is that such women are usually married to partners who are also highly qualified and who are already under heavy pressure to work long hours, travel frequently and widely, and to be on call to function in crises. Similar demands would be made on the wife were she to accept a comparable post and it is the rare family in which both parents can accede to such demands. In East Germany as in the Western countries it is the woman under these circumstances who elects to abjure a managerial position in favor of a more routine assignment.

While the underuse of women can thus in part be ascribed to their own choices, part of the explanation lies with the tardy and inflexible way in which the economic system itself reacts to the facts of women's employment. Although women return to work at about thirty years of age and thus have a long work life ahead of them, little orientation, counseling, schooling, or training is available to them at this point. In the United States a few universities offer the academic woman refresher courses and part-time adult enrollment in regular degree programs, and some community colleges do the same for paraprofessionals. In European countries (except for Scandinavia) and in Japan such possibilities are almost nonexistent. Australia's training programs for adult women provide aid to many women wishing to complete formal schooling, but this assistance is limited to one year and thus better tailored to short-term vocational training than to academic programs. The anomaly is that, although higher education tends to produce more women interested in pursuing careers than is true of the lower levels of preparation, it does little to prepare women for the interrupted careers they are likely to experience or to provide means of completing unfinished education or refreshing stale or outmoded training.

VI. Equal Pay

Although the doctrine of equal pay for equal work is widely accepted and even legislated, it alone cannot guarantee equal opportunity. So long as women's schooling, training opportunities, and skill levels remain below those of comparable men, so long will women remain in the low-skilled, poorly paying jobs, mainly designated for women. So long as employers generally believe that women are poor training investments, that their "career value" is low, that they are unable to perform as supervisors and managers, women's opportunities will be limited to the low-paid jobs, in many of which there are no men to be equal to. In all of these categories and in a majority of jobs that women perform in the labor force, equal pay has little or no practical application. Women's incomes in every country fall below those of men.

"Equal pay for equal work" has an appealing simplicity — so appealing that it has been almost irresistible to legislators in the past few years. Of the countries visited, only Australia had not fully adopted the doctrine. There it is accepted in wage awards falling under the federal jurisdiction but not yet under every state jurisdiction.

Yet nowhere does the adoption of the doctrine of equal pay produce a balance between men's and women's incomes. Part of the wide, and in many countries growing, differential derives from the fact that typical women's work has been segregated from men's and traditionally been priced at lower rates. Some part of it is due to the lag in seniority between men and women of the same age, where women have been out of the labor market for several years. Some find its cause in the fact that many more women than men work part time; and much is attributable to the scanty distribution of women in the better paid jobs. But when they take account of all these and other variables, both Sawhill and Suter and Miller find that a substantial differential still obtains that can be accounted for only by discrimination.

In Sweden women's average hourly earnings in manufacturing have risen slowly during twenty years from about 66 percent of men's to about 87 percent, a far better showing than in most countries but still short of equality. Swedish women working in food and tobacco industries earn 87.2 percent of men's incomes, in textiles 80.6 percent, in metals and engineering 82.7 percent. In Germany, however, the average earnings of women in factories in 1972 were still 31 percent under those of men, and in white-collar employment 39 percent below men's.

Australian figures vary only to the disadvantage of women. Just over 94 percent of women earn under $4,000 per year while the percentage for men is 65.4 percent. Male high school graduates have a median income of $3,780, women of $2,370. The mean income for all men on wages and salaries is $3,090, while for women it is $1,500, according to a 1973 study done by the Commonwealth Department of Labour.

Austrian income tax statistics show that women's incomes average 61.3 percent of men's. As for Israel, in 1973, the *Statistical Abstract of Israel* reported that, among urban employees, women's earnings averaged 58 percent of men's.

Unfortunately comparable statistics for the communist countries are not easily come by. Information handed out there is all to the effect that women earn equally with men; sex differences do not exist. St. George estimates, however, that 65 percent of the gross individual income in the USSR is still earned by men although women make up 50 percent of the working population. He might well have added that women have very little part-time employment, are more widely distributed through the occupations, and have only slightly shorter working lives than men.

In the United States in 1974, the average earnings of employed males were $9,717, but of employed females $4,142. In the professions, women earned about 51 percent of men's earnings; women operatives earned a slightly higher percentage (54.5 percent); and women in the service trades received only about 49 percent of what men did. Put another way, 68 percent of all women workers in the United States earned less than $5,000 per year while only about 32 percent of men were in this category. (In 1969 these figures were 70 percent of women and 37 percent of men.)

Equal pay can only affect women's earnings directly and progressively if women are doing the same work that men do. In Australia, for example, a typist is by definition a woman, and industrial justices asked to make "equal pay" awards to them have difficulty in finding the male category with which they can be equalized. The result, not surprisingly, is that their wages remain at a low point, unaffected by judicial dicta. Similarly, in West Germany and Austria, until very recently a "woman's wage" set at something like 20 percent less than comparable male wages was accepted practice.

One line of reasoning to support these disparities rests on the assumption that the man is the family breadwinner and his wage must be set to support a family. On the other hand, women who work are regarded as secondary earners and do not need to receive wages equivalent to men's, no matter what they do. The differentials in Australia based on this reasoning were so wide and of such long standing before the equal pay demands recently began to make themselves felt, that when awards calling for equal pay were handed down, justices at the same time gave employers at least three years or until 1975 to equalize women's pay with that of men's even when men and women are employed on the same work.

In Japan the reasons for the appearance of wide differences between men's and women's incomes in comparable work are rather different and derive from the unique employment and pay systems prevailing there. Women enter the Japanese employment system as men do immediately upon school graduation and usually receive the same starting wage. The system presumably awards wage increments annually on the basis of seniority and to some extent on ability; however, a sharp difference in the amount and frequency of these seniority awards to men and women sets in fairly early in work life so that when women reach thirty the difference between their incomes and those of men who started with them is very wide. A member of the Japan Employers' Association explained to me that women are not expected to earn their keep, since their attention is properly directed to home and family rather than to work. Indeed, industry expects them to think of retirement when they marry, and if not then, certainly when they have children. In practice women are not considered to be part of the lifetime age-education-seniority system; for the few years when they are in the labor market, they are treated, after initial hiring, more like temporary, marginal beneficiaries of the system than as permanent employees.

A second source of resistance to equal pay has been the trade unions, which as often as employers have moved very slowly in supporting or pressing for the implementation of equal pay. (One exception to be discussed shortly is a group of unions that has initiated a program directed toward establishing a more equitable pay system altogether.) Men in all-male trades, or trades in which women have been segregated in lower-paid occupations, are fearful, as trade unionists have always been, that equal pay enforcement might create an oversupply of labor in the skilled trades and thus reduce the effect that scarcity has in maintaining and pushing up high male wages. In fact, because access is chiefly through apprenticeship, it is almost impossible for women to enter these trades. This is particularly true of married women and mothers who come back into the labor force as adults by which time in most countries they are effectively barred from becoming apprentices.

Another historical principle underlying the assignment of higher wages to men than to women has been that heavy work should be paid more than light work. Women had to do light work and only men could do heavy work; hence men deserved more than women. The introduction of the crane and forklift, of earth-moving machinery, and of automated processes generally has taken much of the "heavy work" content out of blue-collar work. Ditchdigging, for example, is no longer an occupation. In fact, the designation "heavy" has vanished over the years from many job descriptions and is therefore invisible in the assignment of wage classification. On the contrary, the descriptive "light work" remains in many categories in which a large majority of women are employed.[1]

Some of the German trade unions have taken steps to reevaluate the traditional factors included in wage setting, and particularly to determine the

---

1. Some of these difficulties arise also in China where equality of men and women is a cardinal revolutionary principle. *Red Flag (Hung Ch'i)*, the official party paper, reported the following on February 1, 1972, in an article entitled "Equal Pay for Equal Work for Men and Women." "It is noteworthy that in some areas at present there still exists the irrational phenomenon of unequal pay for equal work among men and women. For instance for one work day a man gets 10 points while a woman gets 8 points at most. The reasons variously given are that male commune members have a stronger capacity for labor than their female counterparts, that female commune members have a lower technical level than men and so on and so forth. In sum, 'Female commune members are no match for their male counterparts.' ... We can't impose the same farm work on female and male commune members alike in disregard of the former's physiological features and physical power, but the difference in physical strength must not be taken as an excuse for unequal pay for equal work for men and women. The criterion for assessment of pay for labor is the actual amount and quality of labor each commune member does. It is not based on physical strength still less on sexual difference."

degree to which these "light" and "heavy" categories can still be justified.

Wage systems in West Germany, for example, are often spread over a ten-step scale. It is not unusual to find substantially all the women in steps I and II, and all the men in III through X. Several German industrial unions have recently taken the matter to the negotiating table with employers' associations. The hope is that, by agreement between union and associations, experts will make new job classifications and wage assignments. Their approach will be to attach new weights to such elements of job content as noise, repetitiveness, humidity, temperature, precision, and care of machines, in addition to the traditional factors of skill and physical labor. Their findings are to form the basis for a renegotiation of wage scales. Women expect that their jobs will appear more frequently hereafter in the middle and upper ranges of the scale than is presently the case.

By itself, the equal pay doctrine even when it has achieved the status of statute does little to equalize opportunity. To escape its consequences, an employer need only define the job a woman does somewhat differently from the description of it when a man is the operative. I accompanied such an Australian manufacturer through his water-meter factory when he was building his defense against a union charge of his having violated the equal pay award. In his shop in a few processes men and women worked on the same machine, but he found differences in lighting, in location, and in movement of materials that in his view gave the job a different "content" for the two sexes and thus justified a payment of twenty cents or more an hour more to the man than the woman.

Proponents of equal pay legislation want to be sure that the equality called for in the legislation applies to work "of equal value" and cannot be read to require the kind of literal equality in layout or performance that the water-meter manufacturer was attempting to lay down.

On this point the International Labour Organisation (ILO), whose Convention on Equal Remuneration some seventy-eight countries have now ratified, provides unequivocal definitions both of equal pay and of equal work as guidelines to its member nations. Few have hearkened and fewer still have heeded.

Two approaches, both recommended by the ILO, have, however, met with some success. The one has been used in the Scandinavian countries, where chief reliance has been placed on collective bargaining. In those countries, rates of pay set by the unions and employers' associations become the standard wage scales for all workers in the affected categories throughout each country. The governments of both Sweden and Norway early in the 1960s encouraged the collective bargaining partners to make fundamental changes in the historic systems of wage evaluation and classification that had produced wide disparities between men's and women's wages. Government economists and other experts were made available to the bargaining parties. Over a period of years agreement was reached that the low-wage earners, in which category women were a major element, should receive annually a greater rate of increase than workers at the top of the scale. Within five years, rates for jobs had been made uniform for both sexes and the earnings gap had been substantially narrowed, though not eliminated. As noted earlier, women's wages had been raised from something like 65 percent of men's to over 85 percent. In Norway an Equal Pay Commission was set up to follow developments, call attention to new disparities and inequities, and see that equal pay between the sexes is achieved.

The report of Chairperson Kari Vangsnes shows that preference for male workers over female has resulted so often in employers offering rates above the scale to attract males that a substantial wage drift in favor of male workers characterizes the labor market. Vangsnes concludes that the state has insufficiently taken responsibility "for a more direct contribution towards eliminating the pay discrimination against women." But beyond and prerequisite to effective state intervention is the need

> so to change the role of women at work that they will be able to compete with men on equal terms in all fields of employment....Such a development might be accelerated through improvement of the social infrastructure (e.g., by the provision of child-care institutions and other services to families), by changes in working hours and by far-reaching changes in labour market and educational policy (e.g., by placing the education and training of adults on an equal footing with the same services for youth).

Equal pay without equal employment opportunity and sharing of family responsibilities is probably impossible of fulfillment.

The second approach has been by way of law — the intervention of the state, which Vangsnes sees as essential. This has been the way taken in the United States. In 1963 the Equal Pay Act was passed as an amendment to the long-established Fair Labor Standards Act setting maximum working hours and minimum wages. It was shortly followed by the Civil Rights Act (1964) whose Title VII, covering equal employment opportunity, includes women among its beneficiaries.[2] These two laws, which link equal pay with equal employment opportunity, have become the basic instruments of national policy in the United States.

These acts now apply to a very substantial number of women workers. The Equal Pay Act originally applied to nonprofessional workers in the federal jurisdiction (a very high percentage of all wage and salaried workers). It was extended in 1972 to include executives, administrative employees, and professional employees, including those in all educational institutions. Equal opportunity legislation has similarly been extended. Title IX of the Education Amendment (1972) further prohibits sex discrimination in any educational program receiving federal assistance. Title VII of the Civil Rights Act (1964) covers all private employers in the federal jurisdiction. A 1972 amendment extended its coverage to employees of educational institutions and to state and local government employees, and gave additional enforcement powers to its administrators, the Equal Employment Opportunity Commission (EEOC). Executive Order 11246, later amended by Executive Order 11375, prohibits discrimination on the basis of sex in direct federal employment and by federal contractors and subcontractors.

---

2. The inclusion of sex as a prohibited ground for discrimination under the law was an accident. A southern senator who wished to make proposed legislation designed to benefit ethnic minorities, mainly blacks, unacceptable to his colleagues proposed that the bill before them be amended to bar discrimination on the grounds of sex. The bill passed with his amendment. Because administration preparation for enforcement had not included this provision, there was some delay in putting this aspect of the law into full operation and some time had to pass also before women became aware of its meaning and possibilities for them. By 1970, the Equal Employment Opportunity Commission was receiving more than 3,500 complaints a year alleging discrimination against women by employers, unions, and employment agencies.

A key to enforcement under each of these laws or orders is the guidelines issued by the administrative body empowered to enforce the law. They are all explicit in dealing with the issues and definitions that have troubled administrators around the world who have been charged with enforcement of equal pay and equal opportunity regulations.

Most observers of the enforcement of American laws in this area agree that the best administration has been that of equal pay under the Fair Labor Standards Administration (FLSA) with its large experienced staff of enforcement officers located in branch offices throughout the country. A former associate solicitor of the Department of Labor has claimed that

> if women in the 1960s had to rely totally on Title VII to blot out sex discrimination in the workplace, virtually nothing would have been accomplished. Instead with the Equal Pay Act as part of the Fair Labor Standards Act the interest was kept alive in the courts before the days of the Commission's [EEOC] increased power.

The EEOC reference is to the fact that the commission did not receive the enforcement powers it needed to be effective until the 1970s.

In addition to federal legislation, a substantial number of states have passed some form of equality legislation, often in the form of a Human Rights Act. The Civil Rights Act gives these states initial jurisdiction in complaints alleging discriminatory behavior in employment or elsewhere.

Early Supreme Court decisions almost without exception upheld the complaints that these agencies and individual aggrieved women workers brought before it, with the result that a substantial body of judicial decisions supported the interpretations of the various guidelines. Recently, however, the Court has taken a backward turn. Affirmative action, which under some laws is part of the statute and in other cases a sanction imposed under guidelines, is coming more and more under scrutiny in both state and federal courts. The result has been, for example, a limitation of the application of affirmative action in the Office of Federal Contract Compliance (OFCC), and successful challenges to its operation in several state courts where the issues have to do with the rights of women and minorities in cases where the law provides for preferences to veterans or where companies, and often unions, have provided for special seniority rights for blacks and women in order to maintain their employment during periods of layoff. A Supreme Court decision in May 1977 held that "an otherwise neutral, legitimate seniority system does not become unlawful under Title VII simply because it may perpetuate pre-Act discrimination."

Unquestionably the enforcement agencies have been overwhelmed in efforts to process the number of cases before them. For a time toward the end of 1976, enforcement agencies themselves restricted the types of cases with which they would deal and redefined conditions so as to lessen their case loads. With the naming of new administrators in 1977 following the change of administration, they assumed a more aggressive stance, in some cases seeking in new rulings to deal with issues raised by lower courts. It remains to be seen whether these will stand up when challenged before the Supreme Court.

In commenting on the changes under way in the use of affirmative action remedies late in 1976, *Womanpower,* a monthly newsletter on equal opportunity for women, quoted one of its contributors as saying:

The problem is that people often confuse bad enforcement with bad law. The legislation is good as it stands and the old procedures were good. The problem was that the government never followed its own procedures, didn't get the job done or did it badly. In the wake of poor enforcement, both employers and civil rights groups began to find fault with the laws and regulations themselves.

Womanpower continued editorially:

The Department of Labor has not analyzed where its affirmative action efforts have worked and where they have failed. No one has analyzed what investigative procedures work well, what affirmative action plans or procedures have brought good results, whether preaward compliance reviews produce good compliance efforts, whether hiring "quotas" succeed, what upward mobility efforts have worked well.

VII. Home and Mother

Whether married women work or not, they get little assistance with housework from their husbands. When they work, they must still carry the major responsibility for care of home and children.

Virtually every society assumes that the responsibility for home and children is the woman's. The result is that when mothers work, they carry two jobs. Myrdal and Klein called this "women's two roles." Homemaking-cum-motherhood often takes as many hours as does a paid job, and working mothers spend only slightly fewer hours at it than do professional housewives.

One question I asked working mothers in factories and offices was, "How do you manage?" Those in factories often manage by getting up at 4:30 or 5:00 every morning, planning carefully how to use every minute from then until 7:00 or 7:30 when they punch in at the plant, in order to see that children are dressed and readied for school, that they get off, lunch boxes in hand, often to a neighbor before going on to school itself, and that the preschool child is delivered to its caretaker before the mother herself goes off to work on bus or afoot. ("That hour from 4:30 to 5:30 [A.M.] is the only hour I have to myself in one day," one woman reported, "I can get the ironing done."

The routine is reversed in the evening: help the kids with homework, get more housework done, and at last, oh blessed relief, into bed for six hours or so. This is the working mother's day.

Aren't husbands helping more? Don't they really put their backs to it when their wives go to work? The evidence doesn't say so, either in the communist countries or in Sweden or elsewhere. Studies make clear that husbands and children, when they help at all, tend to assist only with selected, often self-selected, tasks and for a very small fraction of the total hours devoted to housekeeping. As the 1972 multinational time budget research in twelve countries amply demonstrates, the husband spends very little more time assisting the wife and mother with household tasks when she works outside the home than when she does not. Even when children are cared for outside the home, it is the mother who makes the arrangements, delivers and picks up the children, and when they are ill stays home to care for them.

Professor Kathryn Walker, perhaps the outstanding student of time-use in United States households, in a study published in 1973 reports that in families where the wife works the husband assists with housework to the extent of one to three hours per day while the employed wife spends between four and eight hours per day on housework. Walker has found differences in the assistance family members give the wife and mother depending on the number of children in the family, the age of the children, and the age of the wife. Some examples show that the range of assistance to the wife is in no way proportionate to her own input.

The husband who devotes three hours to housework per day has a wife who puts six hours into the work of the home. They have two children, one of whom is one year of age; the older child assists for one hour. The employed wife with four children spends six hours a day on housework and has one hour's help from her husband and one and a half hour's help from a teenage child. The working wife with three children, one of whom is an infant, works seven hours a day at housework and has two hours of assistance from her husband. A working woman with three children under eleven years old will work six hours at home; her husband helps for one and a half hours, and each child helps for one hour.

A study by Professor A. Kharchev of Leningrad of women textile workers in three centers in and near Leningrad comes to substantially the same conclusions. Moreover, surveys carried out by the Leipzig Institute for Market Research in East Germany show that husbands on the average have ten hours more free time per week than their working wives. Ingrid Sommerkorn in her study of women's careers in East Germany sums up the situation: "Although the Family Code makes housework the responsibility of both partners it is still done mainly by women."

However much the life-styles of the educated young marrieds in western Europe, the United States, Australia, and even Japan may stress sharing and equal opportunity, they have not yet begun to throw statistical weight. While they may suggest a future trend that in another generation will have penetrated Western life in an influential way, working mothers in the last quarter of the twentieth century are still carrying a double burden.

VIII. Child Care

*The assistance working mothers seek above all
other is child care fitted to their work schedules.*

Because they carry these double loads, working mothers responded to the question, "What kind of help do you most need?" almost without exception by asking first for more and improved child care and then for opportunities to work part time. It was quickly clear in most interviews that they were not thinking only of the preschool child and of so-called child care centers. They were asking for before- and after-school care, for care of sick children, and for some coverage for school vacations and holidays that cannot be meshed with work schedules.

Preschool Care

With the exception of a very few cities in the world (Moscow may be the only one), needs for child care facilities far exceed supply. The working mother will be lucky to find room for her preschool child in an approved or licensed center. To be sure, in Sweden and Israel she will know that as a working mother she gets preference for available places, but in neither of these countries is space for children under two available except in a very limited way. Austria and Hungary for somewhat different reasons meet this problem by providing, in addition to some crèches mainly in the larger cities, a payment to working mothers who remain at home with their infants. Austria's *Karenzjahr* gives a mother about 45 percent of her wages and is paid from the unemployment insurance funds. In Hungary, mothers may remain away from work for a period of up to three years and will receive one-third of the average worker's wage, currently 800 florints, a payment made directly by the state.[1] The amount of payment is admittedly low. Whether it represents something like a woman's net after deducting extra household expenses incurred when she is working, and therefore is a reasonably fair reimbursement of her financial contribution to the family, is questionable. One indicator is the percentage of working mothers who take advantage of the system in preference to finding outside care for their infants. Ferge notes that in Hungary 60 to 70 percent of all eligible women choose to receive child care grants rather than try to find child care facilities. In February 1971, this amounted to 174,000 women or about 10 percent of the female labor force.

In most communist countries women are expected or even urged to return to work at the end of maternity leave, that is, six to eight weeks after childbirth. Many child care centers, particularly those connected with factories, provide some substantial proportion of their space for children under two. In the East German centers I visited, about half of each facility was devoted to infant care.

---

1. A discussion of the effect such leaves may have on labor market policy or in reverse, the effect labor market policy may have on the granting of paid leave, follows in chapter 10.

Sweden also makes some provision for infant care, beginning when parental leave expires. But the Swedish program still falls short of meeting estimated needs not only for infants but for all preschoolers.[2] In Stockholm in 1970 facilities were available to meet approximately 50 percent of the need, but 103 localities provided no places for infants whatsoever. These last were mainly in thinly settled, rural areas and represented a small proportion of the country's preschool children. A parliamentary decision in 1972 provides that

> a medical notice of birth shall be sent from the maternity department in which a child is born to the child care center in the mother's district of residence, and every child shall remain enrolled at the child care center until school starts. The child care center already in practice bears the formal responsibility for the health of pre-school children.

A Child Care Commission, set up in 1970 under the leadership of Bodil Rosengren, issued its report two years later. The recommendations are now being incorporated in local and national statutes. An important part of the report deals with the growing need for day care for children of working parents and makes important proposals for dealing with the special problems of parents on irregular hours or shift work, for the care of sick and handicapped children, and for standardizing quality of care at a high level for all preschoolers whether in day care or in part-time nursery schools.

In Japan, little or no provision is made for children under the age of two and none whatever for infants under ten months. Yet, mothers who do not return to work at the end of the six weeks' postnatal maternity leave will probably lose their jobs under the rigorous demands of the so-called lifetime employment system. The National Telecommunications Corporation has introduced an exceptional program providing for up to three years' child care leave for its women employees, without pay but with guarantee of the job at the end of the leave period. A majority of women use one year's leave. An informant reported that

> of the 70,000 women employed by the company, 5,000 to 6,000 women a year give birth. Of these, 1,500 to 1,800 use the child care leave system. In this year [1973] counting not only the new users of the system but the persons who have continued on leave from the past year, 3,500 women were on child care leave.

But aside from the privileged women of the telephone company, very few private or public organizations have made such provisions and most working mothers in Japan have no alternative but to resign permanently from their jobs to care for their young infants. Not surprisingly, a substantial number of "unregistered," private, unsupervised child care centers have emerged to meet the desperate need of Japan's young mothers, particularly those living in tiny city apartments where there is no room for relatives. In one such center in Tokyo's first ring of suburbs I found twenty children under eighteen months cared for in two tiny rooms on the ground floor of what had once been a shop. Babies were swaddled and laid on shelves, toddlers were confined to a large playpen, open to the outdoors on warm days, but without outdoor play space. Formulas and food were prepared on a gas plate and the cook stood leaning on the playpen to make best use of her eighteen-inch shelf space for prepara-

---

2. Swedish children begin school at seven years of age.

tion. Parents here had to pay full costs of care since no community or voluntary agency subsidies were available. Staff members, both trained and untrained, were miserably paid for ten hours of unremitting work.

Factory Crèches?

Where women's labor is very much in demand, as it is in many of the countries in this study, factories may provide child care centers as an inducement to attract workers. Such was the case in three Australian plants and in many of the new cities in Israel. In East Germany, factory managers and workers' committees are encouraged if not instructed to provide child care centers where the community facilities are inadequate for employees' needs.

A major problem with factory crèches is that of transportation. Where mothers make long journeys to work, as they do in Japan and many other countries where inner-city rents send blue-collar workers to the suburbs for cheaper accommodations, mothers are unwilling to take children to work on public transportation in the rush hours, particularly since a long journey to work lengthens a child's day intolerably. Moreover, the air and surroundings of factories are also frequently undesirable environments for children. (One West Berlin factory was reported to me as bringing mothers and children to work on a company bus which then carries the children further to the city forest, the Gruenewald, for day care, returning the children to the factory in time to pick up their mothers for the return trip home.) The advantages of care at or near the factory are greatest with very young children whose mothers may be able to see them or nurse them during the day, to have lunch with them, and to have immediate information if anything goes wrong.

Unions often oppose factory-provided care on the grounds that the women workers are thereby made too dependent on the employer—they will be reluctant to leave if conditions are poor; they will accept lower wages in order to receive child care as a fringe benefit, and so forth. It is rare therefore to find unions pressing for employer investment in child care facilities.

Generally, women workers themselves prefer care of their children in the neighborhood where the child is never far from home, grows up with neighborhood children, is spared a long journey to work, and, as the child grows older, may be able to get to the center alone or with an older sibling.

Family Day Care

In view of the all-pervasive shortage of space in centers, working mothers everywhere call on relatives and neighbors to help. Unlicensed, informal, unregulated, and merely custodial child care is much more the rule than the exception. As a matter of fact, caring for other women's children has become an important source of income for many women whose own children are small and who cannot themselves leave home to go to work.

As an interim measure some countries are experimenting with regularizing this kind of family care, allowing mothers of young children, under supervision from visiting welfare workers and with assistance from trained nursery staff, to take two to four children into their homes. The Swedish "family day care" is fairly extensive, covering almost twice as many children as are in centers. Australia has experimented in three locations with a comparable program. In Tokyo, where a scheme of this sort was announced, the plan never succeeded in any marked way, perhaps because apartments there are frequently too small to allow mothers to care for more than their own one or two children.

Shift Work

A more difficult problem arises for the many factory workers, nurses, computer operators, and traffic and communications workers who work on shifts. In most countries outside the United States, shift work means rotating shifts. What about child care under these circumstances?

A common answer is for husbands and wives to choose to work on opposite shifts in order to be sure that one adult is at home to receive the children as they come from school, to help them with homework, to provide an evening meal, and to put them to bed.[3] Communist countries provide a good deal of twenty-four-hour care for children of shift workers; such children are with their parents only on weekends. While in the West, hospitals, telephone exchanges, and some factories have set up centers at their work places, mothers for all the reasons noted above, as well as for the special circumstances inherent in rotation of shifts, usually prefer neighborhood care or care in their own homes.

Although a number of exceptional programs are under way or in the experimental stage, public officials and industrial managers by and large do not want to confront the problem of the mother working shift. Frequently their response to questions about what is or can be done is to back away from the issue, saying that probably women ought not to work shifts, or at least not when their children are small; although they must know full well that in public service and industrial trades shift work is the standard way of scheduling work. Child care agencies are equally reluctant to deal with the question. They point to the probably dangerous outcomes for children if institutions were to try to accommodate care to changing shifts and for the most part declare their unwillingness to follow the communist example and provide twenty-four-hour care.

The result is that mothers themselves are left to find their own solutions. Not surprisingly these are more often than not both accidental and unsatisfactory.

Nowhere in the noncommunist countries visited, except Sweden, are either public agencies or private groups facing up to the question. It is a tough one. The Swedish report on preschool children referred to the problems related to shift work as follows:

> Shift-work and inconvenient working hours are becoming increasingly common in the public and private service sector, and in industry.... Demands have been voiced for more flexible hours at the pre-schools. The Commission emphasizes that the employers' and employees' organizations should consider the question of the family's role and the placing of working hours. An attempt should be made to give

---

3. Philip Stone has a chapter in the multinational study *Use of Time* (Alexander Szalai, editor) concerned with comparative time spent on the child care in twelve countries. It shows that in multiple-child families employed women spend from 252.1 minutes in the United States to 311.3 minutes in France, with the average for all countries at 275.7, while employed men spend a high of 173.1 in Yugoslavia to 228.9 minutes per day in France, with the average at 187.3. (The United States figure for men is 208.3.) A housewife in such families spends a maximum of 386.2 (Yugoslavia) to 537.9 (France), with the average at 434.8.

priority to the needs of parents with small children for better working hours. In the long run, this will create better terms for the functioning of families with children. In the short term, the Commission finds it impossible to offer any categorical solutions. However, attempts should be made to adapt shift systems, for instance, to the needs of parents with young children in another way; regular day shifts, later change-overs on the morning shift and 6-hour shifts. The Commission also recommends that local authorities responsible take a generous attitude towards different hours for pre-schools, in all areas where there is a need for this. The Commission proposes experimental activities, with examples of different models for pre-schools and pre-school hours. In places, including the major urban areas, where there is a pronounced need of pre-school facilities open at night, experimental activities of this kind should be arranged as soon as possible. *The pre-school must accept a collision between objectives and reality.* The essential thing is the children's need for a secure environment, as all around a development as possible against the existing background and real assurance to parents in looking after their children while they make their contributions to working life. (emphasis added)

Perhaps new approaches to the problem need to be found, such as caretaking in homes or neighborhoods, prohibition of shift work but not of jobs to parents of small children, guarantees of alternating shifts to the two parents, introduction of steady shifts for parents. Failure to approach the question, while at the same time scheduling rotating shift work as a condition of employment in many industries where predominantly women are hired, can be taken as one measure of the human irresponsibility of the industrial system.

Before- and After-school Care

Another aspect of child care, whose solution, like that of shift schedules, is all too frequently left to individual ingenuity, is care of school-age children before and after school and during school holidays and vacations.

School begins in most countries between eight and nine o'clock, but factory whistles today blow as they did in the nineteenth century at seven. Schools in many European countries and in Israel end at one o'clock in the afternoon. Children come home then for a midday meal and with a schoolbag full of homework assignments to be completed presumably with parental help for the next morning's classes.

For the most part, working mothers meet this situation by entering into agreements with neighbors to see children off to school and to receive them home again. Other children learn to get their own breakfasts and to unlock the house on their return from school. In a few countries, however, the problem has been assumed by local governments and schools. Swedish day care centers often have a section where older children can report in before and after school. All the Scandinavian countries have instituted "park mothers" who supervise children's afternoons outdoors. Israel has several highly successful experiments under way with "full-day schools," that is, schools open all day with voluntary afternoon registration. In Qiryat Gat, 80 percent of the children stay on in school for afternoon programs, which include activities groups, supervised homework, music, outdoor games, and play. The Israeli minister of education promises that within the decade similar programs will be available throughout the country. East Germany now has two principals in each school, one for the traditional academic program, one for the after-school activities of both children and adults. In Tokyo there is one care center for school children to each two primary schools in most city wards.

Holiday Care

Care of children during school vacation calls for an intricate meshing of camp programs with plant vacations of one or both parents. In Australia the fortunate circumstance that Christmas falls in the middle of summer makes the traditional three-week factory closing at that time coincide neatly with a full half of the school vacation. In Europe, it is not uncommon that entire classes spend part of their holidays in school-managed camps. In the communist countries factories frequently sponsor and operate camps or other holiday outings for the children of workers.

Where none of these solutions quite matches the length of school holidays, mothers everywhere try to get extended, unpaid leave until school begins again, or, failing that, they simply quit their jobs, only to look for new employment again in a few weeks. Some of the disadvantageous effects of such practices were described to me by Professor Judith Buber-Agassi, who did an unpublished study of work patterns of women garment workers in Massachusetts, where she found such practices very frequent. Despite the fact that many women had taken these short interruptions and returned to work for the same employer at fairly regular intervals for fifteen years or more, they were listed in their personnel records each time as "terminated" with serious consequences for their pension, vacation, health-plan, and other benefits. Although most of these women were organized in a union that administered both health and pension plans, the union had, so far as she could determine, made no effort to provide for these circumstances.

The Sick Child

No less a problem is the care of children too sick to go to child care centers or to school. The health plans in a number of countries permit the mother, or in a few instances either parent, to take time off from work for the care of a sick family member and to receive the same benefits as though he or she were ill. Germany is considering legislation of this kind. Sweden already has it on a small scale — an allowance of ten days per year for either parent.[4] But in Sweden, another scheme also provides some assistance. City Child Welfare Bureaus are prepared to send a caretaker to a sick child, if it is already attending a public day care center, and care for it at home, so that neither parent need lose time from work.

---

4. In an electronics factory I inquired of the personnel director about his experience with requests for leave of this kind. He stated unequivocally that he would not permit leave to a man on this basis but frequently did so with women. His reason was, "I can't spare the men; women are replaceable." In fact, it is most frequently the woman who takes such leave. Aside from care of the sick being their traditional responsibility, several women in other countries told me that since they earn less than their husbands, the loss for time off is easier for the family to bear when the woman absents herself.

IX. Part-time Work

*When they cannot find child care assistance,
mothers seek part-time work geared to their children's school day and calendar.*

When a mother cannot arrange for child care, she seeks to solve the problem by working part time. She prefers a job that will match as closely as possible the school day and calendar, especially so, if she is a single parent. When the father shares in child care, she seeks a job that will complement his hours.

Office work in many countries seems to adapt more readily than many other occupations to part-time employment. The service trades, particularly food service, have always accommodated to split shifts or part-time work; hospitals frequently have built their nursing and caretaker staffs around a variety of schedules (in the United States, for example, often accommodating almost totally to the individual wishes of trained nurses available for part-time work).[1]

In several of the German states, teachers may not only work part time, but in doing so may accumulate credit toward tenure. Teaching was often referred to, in my interviews, as the ideal work for mothers, mainly because the mother's and the child's day are exactly matched.

It is in the factories that managers are most resistant to introducing part-time schedules. Yet, even here, change and experimentation are beginning to appear. Despite the fact that industrial managers point to the high cost of administration, the paper work required for "double staffing," and the increase in personnel functions of hiring, training, grievance handling, dealing with problems of absenteeism, illness, accidents, and social services, there is a wide variety of experiments in progress particularly in countries where labor is scarce and manufacturers and vendors want to employ unskilled women workers.

Manufacturers in Germany and Japan during the boom set up special factories to which they recruit only part-time women workers. In Japan, industrial plants began to appear in the neighborhoods of big suburban housing developments, where they recruited married women through mailbox leaflets, and collected and delivered them in minibuses for work during school hours.

In response to the pressure of full employment in the male labor market, a number of companies in Australia began to recruit women and to experiment very liberally with part-time schedules. In a candy factory near Melbourne, women had their choice of ten different shifts, seven of which called for twenty

---

1. This flexibility in hospitals is, however, totally lacking in other countries, notably Japan, where the custom of rotating shifts precludes, in the minds of most hospital administrators, the integration of part-time workers on regular schedules. The result is that in Japan more than half of the trained nursing personnel is not working.

to thirty hours of work a week, while three provided various arrangements to cover forty hours a week. (Part-time workers had a pro rata claim on holidays, sick leaves, and other fringe benefits.) About twice as many workers there were on part time as worked a full week. The testimony of supervisors and of the plant manager was that these part-time workers were more enthusiastic about their work and actually produced more per hour than those working full time. No one in this company had reason to wish to change the offering of flexible shifts or to believe that it interfered with productivity.

Another Australian corporation with an all-male personnel staff offered women workers in two of its plants their choice of a number of part-time schemes, all of which the women rejected in favor of their own proposal for a four-day week. The company acceded and was experimentally operating these two plants with women working the four days of their choice. It had not been difficult, they said, to spread the work, so as to achieve full operation through a five-day week. The testimony here again was favorable, although management agreed that at the experimental stage they might be getting a "Hawthorne effect"[2] rather than a final reading on reduction in absenteeism or increase in productivity.

The communist countries do not encourage part-time work, although both East German and Romanian statistics show that about one-third of married women in fact do work part time. Since these statistics do not differentiate for occupation, and since communist managers presumably share the reluctance of their Western counterparts to match factory schedules to part-time workers, so long at least as they are encouraged by official policy not to do so, one can assume that part-time employment is primarily found in the clerical and service trades.

One form of "part-time work" is sanctioned, however, in East Germany. There mothers of three or more children may quit work without loss of pay three-quarters of an hour earlier than their colleagues, thus working an eight-hour day to the standard eight and three-quarters hours. The Histadrut (the Israeli trade union federation, which in addition to its functions of representation of workers operates a number of industries and services) provides also for a shorter workday for employed mothers.

A variation on part-time work in many countries is "flextime," now introduced mainly in offices, particularly government offices. Flextime schemes provide that so long as workers are present for the total standard number of daily hours and during certain central hours of the day, usually from ten to two o'clock, they may choose their time of arrival and departure. Under some schemes, "flextime" covers the weekly schedule and permits under certain circumstances absences of half a day or even more, thus permitting working housewives to do shopping, visit school, or fulfill other motherly obligations while fulfilling a full week's work obligations. (I did not find anyone experimenting with "flextime" in production.)

---

2. When experimental human relations programs were introduced at the Western Electric plant in Hawthorne, Illinois, in the late 1940s, production increased very markedly in the experimental group. A search for the precise cause in improved working conditions led nowhere and the experimenters had to conclude that increased productivity was a product of workers being in a "special group" which was receiving "special attention" rather than for any other reason, hence the "Hawthorne effect."

In the West, resistance to the widespread introduction of part-time schedules comes not only from managers but from unions. Union leaders find women hard to organize in any case, and part-time women workers almost unreachable. They argue, with some merit, that part-time work is a dead end for women workers. It precludes the chance of selection for on-the-job training and certainly for promotion. It is frequently exploitative in that part-time workers may not be eligible to fringe benefits, to vacations, and to seniority or shift increments; also most of the available jobs call for low levels of skill, low standards of performance, and low pay. Some full-time women workers themselves may not welcome part-time colleagues. In Sweden the objection appeared to be that these women in their fewer hours achieved a pace and production level that full-timers could not comfortably sustain over an eight-hour day, and that they thus were perceived as real or potential "rate-busters." In Israel, a clothing-factory manager in Nazareth freely admitted that his part-timers produced a good deal more per hour than his full-time operators. And in Australia full-time telephone operators had only scorn and hostility for women who wanted to come in part time, to "get the money and escape the nervous strain."

But for all its disadvantages, women want part-time work. In their view it is vastly better than no work at all. Not only does it bring in some money, but it has the very positive advantage of keeping them in the world of work, practicing its skills and acquainted with its rules. When they are ready to work full time they are better prepared to do so.

X. Women and Labor Market Policy

Labor market policy in most countries in respect to women and particularly to mothers is marked by ambivalence, indecision, and even contradiction, a circumstance reflected in women's own confusion about their roles as workers and mothers.

"Women's Work"

Most countries implicitly, if not explicitly, as we have seen in chapter 4, perceive certain occupations suitable to women and others unsuitable. The former may be identified as those calling for "finger dexterity" or "nurturing-caring" qualities. Hence, textile trades, nursing, typing, child care, teaching young children, fine-parts assembly, or jobs connected with women's traditional household and social roles such as cleaning and housekeeping, laundry, food service, retail selling, and hairdressing head the list of acceptable women's occupations. In eastern Europe, but not in the West, medicine and dentistry are women's professions. Countries with a recent agricultural tradition where women have historically done field work are not at all averse to having women work as field laborers, road builders, street cleaners, or helpers in the construction trades and in parks and grounds maintenance. The list is by no means uniform, country for country. Nor is it necessarily constructed on the premise that women have unique dexterity—if so, they would be everywhere watchmakers and dentists — or on the premise that they must be protected against heavy labor—else 80 percent of farm laborers would not be women as they are in Japan and Romania.

The norm-setting International Labour Organisation (ILO) has persuaded most countries to ban women from certain occupations, mainly underground mining, and to set limits on the amount of weight lifting women may carry out in the normal course of their work duties. As noted in the discussion of protective legislation below, countries that have enacted statutory limitations of this kind have usually done so categorically for women and minors, but have at the same time made exceptions for occupations like housework, institutional cleaning, and nursing (where lifting of patients is part of the given task). These prohibitions have also importantly contributed to the concepts of appropriate remuneration for "light" and "heavy" work discussed in chapter 6.

The central question is whether the rationale for distinguishing between men's and women's work, which may have operated with some modicum of logic in the early stages of industrialism, should any longer be made to apply. Evidence everywhere accumulates that the old categories are breaking down.

In Sweden, the United States, and Germany, men are moving into child care and primary education; in Australia men are becoming nurses in greater numbers. Sweden's active labor market policy is to broaden the range of women's occupations. The communists have insisted on bringing women massively into the technical and engineering trades. Under labor market pressures, traditional Australia is putting women to work at hard-hat jobs. The United States affirmative action program is aimed to lower and even eliminate the categorical bars. Very recently newswriters have broadcast the information that women are doing underground work in the coal mines, finding it no more dangerous, disagreeable, or incommensurate with their capacities than it is for men and greatly appreciating the high pay that the United Mine Workers has achieved for underground workers. It would be a mistake, however, to see these incidents in any other way than exceptions to a still very widespread limitation on job opportunity for women.

The Yoyo in the Labor Market

Noncommunist countries tend to look upon women outside the traditional women's trades as a reserve work force to be called into the labor market when male labor is scarce and dismissed when it is plentiful, a view long held about blacks in the United States or about foreign workers in Europe. It is a "yoyo" policy. The classic example was the experience of all industrial nations, combatant or noncombatant, in World War II. Women were quickly trained for jobs for which they had until then been considered unfit and for which today, thirty years later, they are considered unsuitable — jobs on railroads, in ship building, in tank and auto assembly, in oil refineries, and as truck drivers.

Under a "yoyo" policy, foreign labor, blacks, and women are easily manipulated auxiliary labor forces, an economic buffer for the male core against the fluctuations of the business cycle. They can be dismissed when the male market loosens, that is, when "surplus" jobs are fewer or when the supply of jobs and males is substantially equal.

A "yoyo" labor policy dare not reckon with the long-range employment of women outside the traditional women's jobs; any significant investment in training is viewed as risky and shortsighted, as is the delineation of career ladders for women. Instead, the long-range reckoning is to count them as "in-and-outers," not to be treated as a permanent part of the labor force.

Under the acute male labor shortage that existed in the boom economies of Germany, Austria, Japan, and Australia, management in desperation imported foreign labor, including large numbers of women, or began tentatively to consider introducing women into men's jobs. Australia was perhaps the most salient example of the latter. When the labor government in 1972–73 lowered immigration quotas in response largely to union pressures for built-in scarcity in the labor market, managements began to turn to women. Unions gave reluctant and often conditional permission for their employment in hard-hat jobs with the tacit understanding on the part of government, management, unions, and women that, should the market ease with a downswing in the economy or with a relaxation of the stringent immigration policy, women would, of course, go home.

For all the obvious mounting social costs of importing foreign labor in the European economies, only Sweden has decided to turn aside from such a policy and to give priority to recruiting and training its own married women over further support for in-migration of outsiders. Implicit in the Swedish decision is that women should be considered permanent additions to the labor force with appropriate investment in long-range training and placement.

Women's Segregated Labor Market

To the extent that women are restricted to a short list of occupations and are, outside that realm, treated as temporary workers, they constitute a specialized labor market. Yet most labor market reports and measurements make little reference to the differences characteristic of male and female employment. To the degree that effective bars prevent women from entering certain occupations in more than token numbers, the male labor market can be very tight indeed at the same time that the supply of women workers or would-be workers is adequate or even in a surplus. Under these pressures of varying supply, male wages may rise much more rapidly than female wages.[1] Where skill and training are requisites for men's work, women with neither are not directly substitutable for men no matter how severe the shortage. Either job content is fractionalized into simple processes or substitutability occurs at the very bottom of the skill scale, with the effect that men move up the skill ladder as women replace them on its lower rungs.

Scholarly and governmental analyses and statistical descriptions very generally discuss and describe a labor market as though its characteristics are those which pertain only to males and therefore disregard the nonmale participants in it. The head of the vocational training division of the Israel Ministry of Labor, for example, in an official statement in 1971 described the ministry's programs and policies in this area. His reference is constantly to the "young man" — his education before the army, the vocational programs in the army, their supplementation after the army, the operation of apprenticeships, and on-the-job training for "him" in and out of industry. He notes that "young men today can get any work...and earn quite a nice salary from the beginning" and that, therefore, they are not sufficiently interested in the available openings for skill training in the metal trades. He is delighted that 20,000 unskilled laborers are attending evening training and education programs. He calls attention to subsidies to employers to provide in-plant training programs and reports on the upgrading of technicians and "practical engineers." In this area, he reports that

> previously there were no women going into this field, but now girls and young women are attending these courses very successfully. *When there is manpower shortage and everyone is searching for workers, women can enter any field in which men are working....* (emphasis added)

His predecessor in 1967 in a similar report had noted with pride the absorption of fourteen women in "industrial male work" at the same rates as their male colleagues, but commented that "it seems to be hard for a single woman to hold out among a male society of workers." A reading of the various member-

---

1. The Norwegian Equal Pay Council's chief has reported with some chagrin that the effect of introducing equal pay measures in the national economy has been apparently to increase the degree of "wage drift" for men. With male labor in short supply there had been for years a tendency for employers to recruit labor by offering rates above the union scale. With the introduction of equal pay for women and the continuing predilection of many employers to prefer men, the "drift" has broadened and accelerated, but for the male market only.

country reports to OECD on the role of women in their economies suggests how widespread is the acceptance of a special female labor market in which women are relegated to segregated jobs and low-skill assignments or are recruited only "when there is a manpower shortage."

The Japanese government, for example, writes:

Advances in work simplification resulting from technological innovation have opened up wide fields for unskilled workers. As the tertiary sector has expanded... new jobs suitable for women have been created.... From the 1960's on, increasing demand for semi-skilled workers and people for monotonous or simple tasks...has opened up jobs for older women.

In commenting on the growth in part-time employment for women, the report further notes that

the advantages of part-time employment are firstly that it is readily compatible with family responsibilities and secondly that most part-time jobs are unskilled. ... A comparatively high proportion of part-time workers are in fields where employment is unstable and only simple tasks are involved.

Interestingly, this same report points with pride to the high level of women's education in Japan, comparable to men's, at least through the secondary level, and to the requirement in that country for "equal pay for equal work."

The OECD report from Australia refers *inter alia* to demands for the "flow-on of equal pay for work of equal value to the estimated 80 percent of women still not receiving it." It further comments that

women are not assumed to have the same right to work as men — the right for women is conditional upon the relative and prior rights of husband, children, family members. Furthermore, a married woman with an employed husband is not eligible for unemployment benefit; nor is she automatically eligible for sickness benefit.... The acknowledged family restrictions accepted by women workers disadvantage them in that they may be forced to accept the offer of employers who see women as cheap labour or alternative labour in times of shortages.

Even the Swedish report notes that the "women's labour market is far more limited than the men's," that in Sweden "there are still great differences between the earnings of men and women," and that "women are often recruited for jobs with low rates of pay and no promotion prospects"; although by 1980, "the policy of bringing married women into the labour market should be fully implemented."

The Interrupted Career

Jobs and careers are everywhere defined in terms of uninterrupted work life; in other words, the typical male career pattern. Yet, if women are to have babies they must interrupt their work with each birth at least for the duration of statutory maternity leave, but frequently (for reasons discussed in chapter 8) for considerably longer periods. The interrupted career is a fact of life for women, as is responsibility for child care when work is resumed. Still, these inescapable matters are almost never and nowhere taken into consideration in manpower planning, in training programs, in the laying out of career ladders, and in the provision of social services.

Sweden again is the exception. With its decision to recruit married women, it chose an integrated labor market–training–social welfare program adapted to women's special needs. These include reentry orientation and counseling, the institution of "adjustment teams" in plants to deal with special problems that may arise there for women, training and placement oppor- tunities for women including in jobs normally hitherto done by men, and on-the-job refresher and retraining schemes. Child care is reimbursed or provided all through the training period: a measure of the intention to fully integrate women into the labor force is the government's commitment to provide 100,000 new child care places by 1980. Although this commitment was made by the socialist government, which was defeated in the 1976 elections, the new conservative-center government fully accepted this pledge. When in 1977 it appeared that the municipalities were falling behind in their plans for fulfilling this goal, the government promised to take any necessary measures to see that it would be met.

Moreover, legislation has been adopted that makes it equally possible and acceptable for men as for women to interrupt their work lives to care for children. Parents share responsibility for child care. Either parent may take paid child care leave for nine months after birth. Either spouse may remain home to care for sick children or other family members with compensation of about 90 percent of pay from the health fund for lost time. Each adult carries his or her own social security account through life, each pays his or her own income tax, and either may receive the child care allowance paid to parents of children under sixteen years of age.

Other countries provide training for mature women, but in most cases there is insufficient comprehension of all the needs arising out of interruption of work. Training, often available only in the standard women's occupations, pays no attention to the needs of the labor market: lots of hairdressing courses result in an oversupply of trained hairdressers in countries with labor short- ages in the primary and secondary areas. In Germany, for instance, a require- ment for admission to a training program is that the woman pursue at a higher level an occupation that she has once held — if she worked once in retailing she is entitled to training only in some aspect of merchandising. The German programs do not include assistance for women whose higher education has been interrupted; the Australian scheme does, but, as we noted earlier, it offers assistance for only one year.

Israel provides an example of linking social needs with those of industry. A substantial portion of government funds for child care institutions is adminis- tered directly by the Women's Bureau of the Labor Ministry so as to assure child care facilities specifically for working mothers.

Some countries, such as Germany, Australia, and Austria, as we have seen, have set up special offices and orientation programs for women ready to return to work, but the woman who has grown up in a society that does not sanction careers for married women is going to abjure any approach that appears to place her under the taboo. Mere availability of jobs will not change women's place in the labor market. A much more thoroughgoing and consist- ent approach to women's working will have to pervade communications chan- nels.

Of the Western countries studied, only Sweden has training programs for mature women that as a matter of policy open up a widening range of occupa- tions to them. Sweden regards reentry into the work force as a decisive moment in a woman's life, a point at which with good planning and little effort she can be made aware of the fact that she has a long work life ahead, that she will probably work during most of it, that investment in even brief training or in completion of schooling can pay off significantly not only in income but in job satisfaction, and that a new start at this juncture could include consideration of a start in a new occupation.

Women as Supervisors

A concomitant of the view that women are intermittent workers is the view that "they do not take work seriously" and are therefore not good objects for training or other investment, and specifically not sound choices for supervisory training. For one thing, they are considered too old at reentry to begin supervisory training; for another, there is the often-quoted view that neither men nor women like to work for a woman. (A fair rule-of-thumb indicator of labor market policy makers' attitudes toward working women, I decided as my interviews progressed, is contained in their views about women as supervisors.)

In Austria, for example, this view is so widely held that neither industry nor government offers a single program in management training for women. The other end of the spectrum is to be found in the communist countries. East Germany places great emphasis on training women for supervision and management in all areas of employment; but, within the communist sphere, Romania, a much more traditional country so far as women are concerned, is not certain that women will not lose their essential femininity if placed in all-male environments. Women, they say, may of course supervise women and direct factories where a majority of workers are women, but they are still reluctant to train women for management in heavy industry. Fogarty and the Rapoports writing on communist society point out:

> In every occupation in Eastern Europe, women's share diminishes the nearer jobs approach top management ... employment agencies have not developed recruitment, training and promotion practices adapted to the life cycle of married women... so far, planned economies have given the housewife low priority.

Women's Confusion

Where labor market policy is confused or inconsistent and does not, therefore, spin off answers to meet women's special needs, women themselves not surprisingly are confused and conflicted about their roles in industrial society. Like all members of society, women are products of their lifelong socialization. Brought up to look upon work as man's domain and to define success for a woman as marrying "a good provider," having children, and being a "good mother," they feel guilty when they find homemaking boring, the constant company of children stultifying, and the dependency relationship to their husbands narrowing. By contrast, work represents companionship with other adults, some degree of economic independence, and, however dull work may be, no more deadening or repetitious than housework itself. Western society expects working mothers to feel and speak apologetically about the fact that they are working, to limit the time they devote to work, and, when they undertake it, to find an altruistic base for it. "I'm only working until we can get a place of our own where it will be better for the kids," or, "so the boy can go to college."

Such women do not seek counseling or look for jobs that in the long run may improve status, prospects, and earnings. They depend on haphazard information about work as it is disseminated through the neighborhood; they learn about jobs that may be available where their friends work, jobs that are close to home, jobs that call for no investment in training and in which earnings will be immediate.

Another factor affecting women's attitude toward work is a comparable lack of systematic information on the availability of child care, its quality, costs, and services. When a woman applies for a job at a plant, the personnel office may ask her whether she has children and, if so, whether she has provided for their care. With only a little sophistication in the labor market, however, she knows that these inquiries do not stem from concern for her or her children but rather for her regular attendance at and attention to work. In rare instances the plant personnel office may have information about available facilities; in even rarer instances the plant may have a child care center.[2] For the most part both the woman applicant and the prospective employer see the problem as one for the mother herself to solve as a condition of getting a job.

Once she gets a job, she thinks of it as short-lived and interruptable, particularly if family demands go beyond her ability to cope. She has already interrupted her work life to have children and she thinks this may very likely be the continuing pattern of work for her. Western society tells her that work is something you do when you don't have enough to do at home, and that work ought to be abandoned when home duties call insistently. The working mother tends therefore to look on the job as a means of achieving short-run, personal goals.

Under the pressures of familial demands and with minimal family assistance in meeting them, the wife and mother regards herself as a secondary, albeit essential, contributor to the family's economic well-being. Similarly, she sees herself as a secondary source of employment and of unusual expense to her employer, a person to be called on when men or young women are not available in sufficient numbers or when the cost of employing men can be reduced by employing women or when high-priced skills can be fractionalized into low-cost, largely mechanized operations, which unskilled workers including women can perform.

Holding these views, as woman have been socialized to do, they come to regard any investment of their own in time or money for training as dysfunctional. They prefer to earn money where and how they can, to change jobs when better opportunities arise, if they ever do, and to drop in and out of work as family pressures dictate. This is, after all, not an unrealistic or illogical conclusion for women to reach, given the world in which they live.

The woman in a communist society, on the other hand, is no less socialized to the opposite view. Forces as pervasive and formative as cigarette and soap advertising in the United States are concentrated on shaping the attitudes of women about work and about women at work. As Dodge points out, "The Soviet Union has succeeded in creating an atmosphere in which a woman feels apologetic if she doesn't work." She assumes that she will work all her adult life with minimally short interruptions for childbearing and child care, and that the state will accept responsibility for child care, including care of very young children, during working hours. Also, the state will provide, she believes, a better quality of education, training, and physical hygiene than she could give her child at home.

---

2. See chapter 8 for attitudes of mothers toward factory child care centers.

As for her double burden in terms of housework, we know very little about how she feels about sharing household tasks with her husband. According to Kharchev, Szalai, and others who have studied time-use in these countries, however, she gets very little help from him or from her children, no more indeed than the Western employed housewife.[3] Moreover, her access to work-simplifying household appliances is still very, very limited; public facilities to assist with such tasks as laundry and heavy cleaning are almost as limited and, where they exist, pretty poor in their performance. These women may not be confused, but they are working to full capacity as the small showing of women representatives in trade union and political posts gives ample testimony. There is little time and energy for the working mother to take a third role, that of community activity.

In the West, a woman's double role results not only in a double burden but in her being quite literally of two minds about work and child care and home. This schizoid self-view contributes to her helplessness, manipulability, and passivity.

What Is to Be Done?

Most of the developed countries have committed themselves to equal pay and equal job opportunity for women. A number have taken substantial strides toward implementing these commitments; a number, still very tradition-bound where women are concerned, have taken refuge in rhetoric.

The motivation for a thoroughgoing and consistent program undoubtedly must derive from strongly held values of human equality, but they must also probably be sustained by economic needs and outcomes. Constitutional clauses, hortatory promises, political platforms, and party programs have not achieved these ends.

It is probably safe to say that across ideological and national boundaries, programs to increase women's employment and encourage their upgrading have for the most part operated on the assumption that women are a reserve labor force. They have been linked to periods of stringency in the male labor market—the war in all combatant countries, the postwar era in those developing economies suffering from a severe male shortage—and are thus pursued with varying degrees of commitment and support. To be sure, these periods have varied considerably in length, from the duration of a war to the two generations necessary to replace a decimated male population. One can speculate that even in East Germany, where the most spectacular and consistent emphasis has been placed in recent years on women's training and promotion, pressures in this direction may relax as the population slowly achieves sex equilibrium in the next few years. The proportion of women working in Russia has in fact decreased as that process has gone on there.

To adopt another view, one operating on the assumption that women will work (for all the reasons outlined in chapter 2) and that they can contribute as

---

3. A report entitled "How Equal Are Soviet Women?" in the *New Statesman* (London) says, "On the domestic side of life, Soviet women have by no means achieved equality. All the women I talked to made no bones about saying that a man's life was the easier.... Lenin's wish for the release of women from 'domestic slavery' is attempted in slowly increasing household automation and in such flourishing housewifely aids as *culinarias* where food is sold already cooked.... The major part of all shopping and housework is still done by women. ... " Jill Tweedie, September 21, 1973.

individuals and not as a sex category to national economy, calls for a very different approach from the one the West has so far at least been ready to put into operation. Several approaches have been initiated, however, and here perhaps Sweden and the United States are the outstanding examples.

The Swedish Model

The Swedish approach has both ideological and economic grounds. On the one hand, the Swedish commitment in social policy to equality not only of the sexes but of young and old, of handicapped and healthy, foreigner and native, rich and poor resulted in a thorough examination during the 1960s of what the Swedes called "sex roles." They see the causes of inequality for women in pay and work as rooted in the sex role imprinting that goes on in the family, in school, and in society at large. A reform of textbooks and curricula, of parent education, child care, tax policy, and marriage and divorce law have accompanied a labor market policy constructed to fit women's special needs as mothers.

Its economic motivation sprang from considerations of the heavy social costs of continuing to import foreign labor and the decision made about 1965 that the reserve pool of married women in Sweden constituted a readier and less costly source of labor supply. The Swedes were clear that the cost of mobilizing this labor reserve would not and should not be cheap. Women were not to be employed at lower wages or under restricted conditions. If they were to be called up, it was to be as workers enjoying the full benefits of all aspects of Swedish labor market policy: training, counseling, rational placement, integration in the full range of occupations. It involved a reevaluation of wage policy, a task that the unions and management organizations had to undertake, but for which government research and other expert assistance were available.

Specifically, a woman reporting to a labor office who had previously worked was to be immediately counted as unemployed and therefore eligible to an unemployment benefit until she found work. She was counseled to undertake a training program and her abilities and experience were evaluated and assessed as the basis for a grant-in-aid of such training, whether it would take a few weeks or several years. Supplementary aid for transportation, fees, texts, and tuition was available. More important, child care costs or facilities were at her disposal. She was directed to prospective employers and given travel money for interviews if that was needed. If she found a job away from her present home, she was assisted with moving expenses to reach her new destination and helped in finding housing and child care there. In short, there is thorough coverage of the cost of preparing for work and expenses of relocating if necessary.[4] The Swedes estimate, however, that within four years, such a woman, in addition to contributing to her own support and that of her family, is making a positive contribution to the economy in terms of productivity and to the state in taxable income. Within a relatively short period she has more than paid off the investment made in putting her to work.

An informant described the working out of the program by letter in 1974.

---

4. These programs are equally available to men and to women. By the end of 1972 the Labor Market Board deemed that the service for women was sufficiently understood by the public and its district staffs that the special women's division of the board could be abandoned.

Introduction of the separate tax return as of 1970 was meant to bring married women into the labor market in lieu of aliens. It did, but at the wrong moment: there was a downturn in the demand for workers in 1971, 1972 and the first half of 1973, which caused a considerable increase in the numbers of unemployed workers in general and female job seekers in particular who could not be placed. Young people entering the labor market were also badly hit.

Therefore, as part of regional development, employers were promised a substantial subsidy toward the wages of women and adolescents being trained on the job. It came to something like 5,000 kronor per employee during six months to a year.

Next came the extension of governmental loans and grants to industries being established or expanded in geographical areas which require industrial development. These loans were made contingent on at least 40% of the workforce being of the sex which is in the minority in the industry in question.

Last, but not least, the Labor Market Agency or rather its district offices are now stepping up experiments with so-called "adjustment teams," consisting of agency officers, trade union representatives, representatives of the management and employees of the plant which is to be "adjusted." *This team studies the operation of an enterprise or plant with a view to adjusting the work process to the capabilities of the locally available manpower.* (The tide in the labor market has turned, companies are looking for workers, but management wants first-rate young men—from abroad if they cannot find them in Sweden—while the labor offices have applicants on their hands who do not meet the employers' specification: women — a recent report showed that of some 70,000 people who say they would accept employment if there were any (latent job seekers, we call them) 10,000 are women — older people, handicapped persons.) Adjustment may consist in a vast variety of measures: dividing one job into two part-time jobs, reducing strain, etc. (emphasis added)

A visit to Sweden in 1977 showed that all of these programs are in operation. Indeed, the subsidy available to employers for training or retraining women on the job has been increased. In plants whose location out of crowded areas is supported by regional development subsidies, the condition is that the work force represent at least a 40/60 balance of the sexes. This requirement can be waived or modified only in cases where employers show that a good faith effort in recruitment has been unsuccessful.

An important part of the Swedish program is clearly not just recruitment, training, and placement, but follow-up of an innovative kind—the adjustment of the job to the worker, including the woman worker.

The United States Model

In the United States a similar ideological commitment to equal opportunity was focused particularly on ethnic minorities, mainly blacks, who were by the year 1964, when the Civil Rights Act was in draft, perceived to be in greatly disadvantaged positions as to schooling and especially job training. In a political maneuver designed to obstruct passage of the bill, a senator opposed to its intent amended it to include women. The bill nevertheless passed the Congress including in its provisions sanctions on discrimination against women in employment. A year earlier an equal pay bill had been passed. These two pieces of legislation have had the effect of giving women access to enforcement agencies and the courts in their efforts to combat discrimination both in pay and employment and to benefit by administrative guidelines as well as court decisions, which have over the intervening years more and more sharply defined both goals and enforcement procedures.

Neither Sweden nor the United States in this period since 1965 has fully succeeded in eliminating labor market discrimination against women, nor in completely changing social biases and traditions that operate with great power on all the actors in the labor market — workers, employers, unions, schools, training institutions. Nevertheless, substantial changes have been made and the road is open.

A Labor Market Policy for Women

A special labor market policy for women is crucial to making productive workers out of women as well as enabling them to live tolerable working lives. To continue to make labor market policy as though "worker" is a masculine noun is to overlook and disregard the basic differences in women's lives. Because of interruptions for childbearing, many women arrive late (measured by male norms) in the labor market. In addition, they must cope, without training and counseling facilities, with the failure to gear what facilities there are to women's schedules. To demand that women make up for those differences on their own time and at their own expense is to increase their already heavy burdens intolerably. The effect is to condemn them to second-class industrial citizenship.

Many writers, including Professor Galenson in her survey of women at work in a number of countries, believe that women can make it to equal status under the present rules *"if they want to."* My view is that they neither can nor will, given the nature of their adult life cycle, the weight of traditional pressure on them to perform the child-caring and homemaking roles, and the ambivalent and discriminatory policies controlling their access to work. Labor market policy must explicitly recognize their special circumstances and needs and social welfare policy must be organized to provide the necessary support.

XI. Protective Legislation

Protective legislation, the historic response to meeting women's special needs, not only may operate to discriminate against women as workers, it also rarely adequately assists them with their unique maternal functions.

Protective Legislation: Discrimination?

Historically the special regard society has given working women has been expressed in protective legislation, for example, prohibiting certain operations, exposures, and locations to women. The ILO has over the years of its functioning adopted a number of conventions which member nations were expected to ratify as part of their respective national labor codes. These have covered, among other restrictions on women's work, prohibitions against night work, lifting weights above fifteen or twenty pounds, and underground work. Most of the noncommunist nations subscribe to these conventions; the communist ones on the whole do not, nor does the United States for its own reasons, although both follow some of them selectively.

Within the past decade, substantial opposition has arisen in a number of countries, including Sweden and the United States, to the application of such prohibitions to women as a class.

The arguments for their abrogation run along two lines. First, nations have made very broad exceptions to the laws where public convenience or safety is involved without regard to the health or convenience of the women workers concerned. Examples are the lifting of night-work prohibitions for telephone operators, women in the entertainment trades, nurses, and women doing cleaning and servicing of public buildings. Second, categorical prohibitions on women working nights tend to bar women from jobs that pay a night-shift differential and to discriminate against them in a free labor market for jobs that include night work.

Recently, in publications of the ILO itself observations have appeared that suggest that reconsideration of these conventions is not far off. A redrafting of them could well take the form of calling for protection of individuals who for any reason need such protections. They would include many physically handicapped, elderly, and young persons rather than the female sex or any other group categorically. Sweden has already adopted legislation based on this approach. The United States, if and when the Equal Rights Amendment is ratified, will have nullified all categorical legislation by sex. The communist nations have long since moved in the direction of equal rights and duties at the work place regardless of sex. On the other hand, some nations, and here Japan is notable, attach great importance not only to continuing but to strengthening special protection for women workers. Union programs there call for longer maternity leave, longer nursing periods, mandatory menstrual leave, and more stringent enforcements of night-work prohibitions. In a country where women are as severely disadvantaged as they are in Japan, it is not surprising that they see their best hope of immediate help in terms of extended categorical statutory protection.

Maternity and Child Care Leaves

One category of protective legislation, however, must still be guarded, extended, and enforced. These are the statutory benefits and protections for women during prenatal and postnatal weeks, and provisions for care of newly born infants. Most nations, whether or not they accept responsibility for protective legislation for women as a class, nevertheless write maternity benefit legislation. (The United States is one of the few exceptions.) These laws usually originate, however, not from consideration of women as workers but of women as mothers and they are drafted and administered in the welfare rather than in the labor ministries. Typically they provide for regular physical examinations of the mother, prenatally and postnatally; leaves from work at least twice daily to nurse infants; and care of the healthy as well as the sick or handicapped infant through its first year or even until the child is enrolled in school. They may cover all or part of in-hospital delivery costs and often include a one-time grant to provide a layette. They may call for a designated amount of time off for the working mother before delivery and usually provide for paid leave for some weeks after delivery as a health benefit. In Japan, employers must pay for the pre- and post-natal leaves; generally, however, these are charges on the respective health insurance system.

Much rarer is the provision of child care leave for a parent after birth, and rarer still is any scheme for paying a parent a sum in lieu of wages for remaining at home to care for an infant. For women who have to work, child care leave without pay may be an unattainable luxury; even for the family of middle income it means long planning in advance and the assumption of a heavy personal burden. In Japan, where interruption of work beyond the limits of postnatal leave often means loss of the job itself, the provision that some companies (notably the National Telecommunications Corporation, referred to in chapter 8) make for unpaid leave of up to three years with guarantee of the job on return to work is a significant advance.

Austria and Hungary provide for paid child care leave; and most communist countries, while not providing paid leave, give women up to a year's unpaid leave when a child is born with uninterrupted credit toward retirement. East Germany actually shortens a woman's required years of eligibility for pension by one year for each child born. Thus the year a mother may spend at home with her infant does not interrupt her accumulation of pension rights; on the contrary, such leave accrues toward fulfillment of those requirements.

In Sweden either spouse may apply for child care leave, depending on family circumstances and the preference of both parents. That it is more frequently the mother than the father who stays home is often a product of the mother's lower level of earnings as well as of the traditional view that the child will receive better care from the mother than the father. Many examples of fathers taking child care leave exist however.

The United States is the only major industrial nation in 1978 without a national health insurance plan covering medical expenses including those for childbirth, to say nothing of compensation for lost income. Most U.S. workers covered by health insurance are enrolled in private plans negotiated and managed by their union and their employer. Maternity benefits under private insurance plans usually provide no more than a flat-sum payment toward hospital costs. As of this writing only five states provide for any disability payments for lost salary during illness and of these only four have included payment for disability resulting from pregnancy. In 1974 the Supreme Court sustained a California state court, which had ruled that the failure of the California disability law to pay for pregnancy was not sex discrimination. In 1976 the Court declared that pregnancy was a unique condition that employers are not required to treat as an insured disability. This decision in effect nullified the ruling of every federal court that had considered the matter as well as the EEOC ruling that the exclusion of pregnancy from coverage was illegal sex discrimination. To correct these circumstances, a Pregnancy Disability Act amending Title VII of the Civil Rights Act was introduced in Congress in 1977. The bill would require employers to cover pregnant workers under temporary disability and health insurance plans and would prohibit discrimination against pregnant women in all other aspects of employment.

We have the anomaly in the United States that protective legislation was written to protect women as future mothers from overexertion and exposure to noxious or exhausting labor; in fact, as we have come to see, it mainly has helped to reinforce woman's isolation from the mainstream of productive labor and handicapped her in receiving equal benefits from it. On the other hand, her special and unchanging function of bearing children has not been supported financially nor has she been aided or encouraged to take care of her infants because taking child care leave has meant certain loss of pay and perhaps even loss of job.

As suggested above, it is doubtful that the philosophy underlying maternity and child care leave where it does exist springs from consideration so much of the mother as of the child. If the mother were a major object of concern her need for income during leave would have to be considered. For women who have to work, the provision of a cash benefit in lieu of wages makes the difference between their being able to take the leave and having to forgo full use of it. The effect of child care leave on working mothers who can use it is to give them periods of rest and time for devoting themselves to their children and to their own well-being. The knowledge that job, seniority, pension, and vacation rights await them on their return to work is vastly reassuring.

XII. Social Welfare and Social Insurance

Social policy covering retirement, health plans, and other welfare programs for women is confused and contradictory, often treating women as spouses to their disadvantage as workers.

In every industrial country but the United States, as we have noted, health insurance programs are available under governmental or quasi-governmental auspices. If they are not supported by national contributions, they are closely regulated by law. Many of these programs, particularly those in central Europe, trace their histories into the nineteenth century. The British health insurance scheme is a product of the 1920s. These dates suggest that the contributions and benefits are set up on the assumption that the breadwinner is a male head of a family, that he is the chief beneficiary, and that his wife will receive secondary benefits, if she is covered at all. Some laws exempt companies employing women from insuring them if they are already covered by husbands' policies. Under some regulations, women who are heads of households or whose husbands are unemployed find difficulty in getting primary coverage. Under these schemes women are often additionally handicapped unless they are able to show continuous work experience covering a required number of months or years for eligibility to some or all of the benefits.

Similarly, with retirement plans, women have customarily been regarded more as spouses or widows of retirees than as retired workers on their own account. In some cases their own accumulated earnings over the years have been so low or so intermittently received that they fare better as widows in accepting a widow's pension than one to which they might be eligible on their own behalf. Women widowed in middle age often are too young for widows' pensions and have therefore to go to work for the first time in their forties and fifties. For such women the total period of employment can be insufficient to achieve eligibility to pensions in their own right.

In some countries, notably the United States until very recently, a considerable number of women's occupations simply were not eligible for any kind of social insurance. Among these were farm labor and domestic services. In the early years of the United States system, survivor benefits were not available to children of a working wife when her husband was present. Nor were benefits payable to the husband or widower of a working wife. In the United States these matters have been corrected, though change did not come until 1967. And only in 1973 did widows become entitled to 100 percent of their pensioner husbands' benefits. Until that time they had had to be content with a fractional payment. With the increasing number of women workers, the American program has had to deal with the problem of the woman eligible to dual benefits—on her own account and as a widow. In this case, she now receives first her own benefits, and then, if her rights as a widow entitle her to more, she receives a supplement to bring her income up to the larger amount.

Although 90 percent or more of American workers are now covered by Social Security, the system still operates regressively for women. Probably 95 to 96 percent of women are paying Social Security tax on their total earnings, whereas considerably less than 85 percent of working men do so. For low-wage families, and here families headed by women make up an undue proportion, the sums paid in Social Security taxes exceed the sums paid as personal income taxes.

"No national legislation or international instrument yet places husband and wife on an equal footing in respect of survivors' rights," reports Pierre Laroque in his summary study "Women's Rights and Widows' Pensions" (1972).

> The essential problem here is to get away from any notion of a right attached to widowhood as such ... and so to eliminate as far as possible the principle of a woman's dependence on her husband. A woman, like a man, should in all circumstances have a personal right to an old age pension. ... This is true of the basic pensions of the Scandinavian countries.

In most countries women are entitled to retirement at a somewhat earlier age than men—in the United States, this is sixty-two as compared with men's eligibility at sixty-five. In most European countries a woman may retire five years earlier than a man. But, in circumstances where salary increases with seniority and where pensions are related to total or average salary, this earlier retirement may disadvantage women who are already, in all probability, entitled to less than men since on the whole their incomes tend to be less and their total earnings over a lifetime are almost certainly less.

In West Germany, for example, a pension should represent 60 percent of preretirement earnings after forty years of insurance. As Dalmer Hoskins reports, "Benefits directly reflect the level of earnings and length of coverage. There is no 'bending' of the formula in favor of those with low earnings records. There is a maximum pension ... but no provisions for a minimum." West German women do, however, receive rather generous credits for certain periods when they are absent from work, including leaves for extended illness and maternity, periods spent in educational institutions, and apprenticeships after the age of sixteen, but, "reflecting the lower average earnings of women, the tables differ according to sex, with lower contributions being credited to insured women than men." It is not surprising therefore that the average retirement pension for women is considerably less than half the amount received by men. The difference is accounted for by the shorter average length of insured coverage of women and their lower average earnings.

A new marriage and divorce law went into effect in West Germany on July 1, 1977, which regards the two partners as equal contributors to the marriage. In the case of divorce, each spouse has the right to half the pension benefits derived from contributions paid during the marriage, whether by one or both spouses. A number of other proposals affecting social insurance are due for early consideration. One is to give an insured woman an additional year of insurance credit for each child to which she gives birth, as partial compensation for her dropout from employment to care for children. This might be based either on an average of her earnings or on a national average of wages and salaries. The plan also calls for a reevaluation of retirement benefits of persons with twenty-five years of coverage who are receiving low pensions. The problem is that the requirement of twenty-five years of insurance excludes many women, perhaps some of the ones most in need of supplement. The German Trade Union Federation (DGB) has proposed a special "hardship" allowance to women retirees whose earnings records are below the national average.

In the communist countries, pensions are for the most part paid directly from the government budget. Women retire five years earlier than men, but usually both men and women receive the same flat sum, to which they are eligible if they have worked a given number of years. East Germany experts whom I consulted spoke with pride of the recent increase of this pension to about 250 East German marks per month, less than half of the average monthly income. All retirees are encouraged to continue working, and, should they elect to do so, their pensions are in no way negatively affected. Observations through my trip there suggested that a high percentage of retired men and women in fact do continue working. Indeed, given the present rate of pension payment, it is probably necessary that self-supporting persons do so. One feels compelled to consider whether, like the fixed low wage, this pension policy is not a labor market device to retain the working services of able-bodied older workers, while permitting the infirm to retire on pension-supplemented health insurance payments.

In the communist states, where pensions are not related to previous earnings or years of work, women do not suffer peculiar disadvantage as a result of earlier retirement or interrrupted work life. They receive as much as men who work five years longer. An East German pension expert explained that the state finds the justification for what may appear as an inequity to men in the fact that women, all their working lives, have worked harder than men by carrying family and child-rearing responsibilities while they were employed.

In Japan where women not only retire legally five years before men—the respective ages there are fifty and fifty-five — but are customarily urged to retire at very early ages (usually around thirty in private industry), and where retirement is a company benefit paid in a lump sum accrued on the basis of about 2 percent of salary per year of work, early retirement, when it coincides with marriage, may actually have considerable appeal to a woman, who in effect receives a lump-sum marriage settlement. Women's problems under this system arise when they desire at some later date to find new employment — they have no legal or customary claim on former employment once it is terminated. The adult labor market exists only in the "secondary level of the economy" under terms of casual employment, usually without a labor contract and with few if any benefits, certainly none for retirement and rarely any for health insurance.

It is apparent that the characteristics that describe women's employment generally—interrupted and shortened work lives, jobs at low skill and low pay—accumulate to the heightened disadvantage of the woman worker in her disability and retirement. The Scandinavian experience of treating each individual as an entity in the insurance system has the effect of insuring women both in and out of the labor force for a continuous individual lifetime account. The Germans' reevaluation of their retirement system shares many of these concerns and appears moving in the direction of the Scandinavian model.

XIII. Women and Trade Unions

The proportion of working women who are members of unions is far lower than is the case with men, in part because such advantages as adhere to union membership are less available to women than to men. Women are often working in industries that have never or only marginally accepted organization. Even when they are organized, union scales and rates in many industries and nations still give women lower rates of pay, fewer or less-advantageous fringe benefits, and in some instances exclude them from a wide range of occupations – almost invariably those with the highest rates of pay. As members of unions, women typically play a minor role in leadership and appear as token representatives in the executive boards rather than in proportion to their membership numbers. Union programs do not typically put women's issues at the top of their agendas.

Assuming that trade unions on the whole succeed in getting higher wages, better working conditions, and more fringe benefits such as health insurance and paid vacations for their members than unorganized workers are able to achieve, then workers who are not union members or not covered by union agreements are by comparison disadvantaged.[1] Women in most countries fall significantly into this category. The percentage of women workers in every country who are members of trade unions is lower than the percentage of men, and women are a decided and disproportionate minority in unions' decision-making bodies whether in the communist or the noncommunist world.

Historically unions were organizations predominantly of men. To the extent that they were in their origins organizations of skilled workers, only very exceptionally were women eligible for apprenticeships and hence to member-

---

1. Labor economists on the whole agree with Clark Kerr's. analysis in "Trade Unionism and Distributive Shares" that, despite the pressures and programs of trade unionism over the past forty years in the United States, labor's share of the gross national product has not changed very much. "The power of trade unionism has been apparently countervailing and not original." On the other hand, among workers, those who are organized tend to have higher wages than those who are not. If labor's total share of GNP has not increased, this would mean that nonunion workers get less than their share and specifically that women, who are so predominantly unorganized, are in this respect additionally disadvantaged. In Britain and Sweden, on the other hand, through what might be viewed as original political power, unions can be said to be responsible for a significant redistribution of income.

ship. Early organizations of workers in most industrial countries tended to be in mining, the most exploited and dangerous trade (where women when they were employed took the place of mules, hauling the coal cars or coal sacks along the mine alleys for delivery at the surface) and printing, the most educated (into whose ranks women with their deficient schooling or total illiteracy could not enter).

Still, women and children entered industry at least as early as men did—they were employed in textile mills from the beginning—and in some countries were the first industrial employees. Japan provides perhaps the most dramatic example of women's central role in the early stages of industrialization. In the late nineteenth and early twentieth centuries, textiles were the major industry and textile products the major export. As such they were the source of foreign exchange, which in turn was used to capitalize and equip the heavy industry, especially munitions. Thus it was women's labor in Japan that provided the funds that built the foundation of the country as a modern industrial power.

In spite of women's early appearance in industry, the history of women's organization into unions is everywhere sporadic. Japanese textile workers had no union until after World War II. The Lowell girls in the 1840s and the Lawrence strike in 1913 in the United States, the uprisings of Belgian and German textile workers in the mid- and late nineteenth century, and the history of British trade unionism provide at most dramatic episodes of women's trade union militancy. Overall, women not only were not organized but indeed were used to break down standards that men had painfully achieved.

G. D. H. Cole sums up nineteenth-century history in England on this matter.

> It was impossible for the working classes of the early 19th century to devise a policy at once practical and constructive. They were too weak. In the manufacturing districts the machine was steadily dispensing with the old craftmen's skill and enrolling women and children as machine minders or to beat down the wages of the man.

The conclusion of the classic historians of trade unionism, Sidney and Beatrice Webb, that most organizations of women trade unionists in Great Britain were "ephemeral" applies indeed to the history of women workers generally.

The early unions in most countries were craft organizations of highly skilled, locally resident male workers with a lifetime commitment to their trades. They throve on labor scarcity and sought not to include every worker, but rather to exclude all, male or female, for whom they could not reasonably expect to provide work in the area. With the appearance of industrial unions, which are inclusive organizations relying on numbers rather than on artificial scarcity of skill for their bargaining power, women were welcome to the extent they were part of the work force. Industrial union history in most countries takes on significance from the immediate prewar period, and this form of organization became general after World War II. In Britain and the United States, where trade union history was not radically interrupted by the war, there are still both craft and industrial unions.

But even the industrial unions, with their acceptance of women, have not been strong or original advocates of women's equality in work life. The support that they have given to improving women's conditions has largely been to set a floor under their wage exploitation, making them less attractive to employers who might want to use them as substitutes for more expensive male workers. Thus, unions have tended to support minimum wages for women, the control or outright abolition of home work, the institution of protective legislation, and the banning of women from such occupations as underground mining.

In practice, unions have tended to accept segregation of women into certain auxiliary jobs such as bookbinding in the printing trades; serving as cashiers and wrappers for butcher workmen; topping, seaming, and inspecting in full-fashioned hosiery; mending in the lace-making industry; serving as telephone operators but not installers in communications; sewing but not cutting or pressing in the garment trades. In doing so they have frequently agreed to set up discrete parallel wage and seniority rosters for men and women, with no crossing of lines and with differentiated wages scales. The craft unions have simply not accepted women for apprenticeships in such skilled trades as those of machinist, millwright, carpenter, electrician, sheet-metal worker, lather, railroad engineer, truck driver, or airline pilot, thus effectively barring these skilled occupations to women.

Is women's membership in unions small because union policy and practice have tended to leave them out of certain trades and occupations? Or is it because men regarded them as unpredictable and uncertain additions to union rolls? Or are their small numbers their response to union policies that call for relatively high dues and offer, as women see them, uncertain or negligible benefits?

In Sweden, although nearly 40 percent of the labor force are women, they make up only 25 percent of the total trade union membership. Similarly, women in Japan are 38 percent of the work force and only 28 percent of its union members. In West Germany, where women are over one-third of the labor force, only 20 percent belong to unions, and in the United States only about 16 percent of all women workers are union members whereas something like 28 percent of all men workers belong to unions. Comparable figures are not available for the communist countries. They claim that 98 percent of the workers are members of their unions, and, since unions for the most part administer the social security systems in these countries, it is altogether likely that nearly all workers belong to their trade union organization in order to receive these benefits, if indeed they have any choice in the matter. For similar reasons the trade union participation rate for women in Israel is relatively high.

Women's Role in the Unions

Some unions are made up almost entirely of women. The textile and garment trades around the world are cases in point. Almost nowhere, however, are the leaders of these organizations women. The same can be said with almost as much general force for unions of white-collar workers, an occupation that employs more women than any other in the industrial societies. What is the explanation? One observation is that in the industrial unions, leadership is more often than not drawn from the more highly skilled elements of the membership. Since women are rarely in these echelons, their exceptional presence in union executive bodies could be seen as part of this process of natural selection. Where they are in a minority, as they often are in heavy industry, the likelihood of their emergence in the upper ranks of leadership is even less. A common belief among female as well as male unionists is that women prefer to be represented by men rather than women, particularly during the crunch of hard bargaining in contract negotiations. On the one hand, they say that women do not trust their own power and skills at these crucial periods and, on the other, men have more clout with the male employers.

In most countries in Europe and Asia, however, women are not altogether invisible. Union structure in these countries provides for a women's division at each level of each organization and these divisions are often, though not invariably, headed by women. Typically, a women's division chief is the only woman in the union executive and the section that she heads is usually overburdened with problems of organization, administration, education, and social services within the union, including thus both functions for women and the secretarial and social tasks usually accepted as women's functions among its tasks. Almost never, however, does the division's chief appear at the bargaining table or participate in or plan legislative and political action, the central activities of unions in the noncommunist world.

Communist unions too have women's divisions and union executive bodies almost always include at least the woman who heads the division. But women are rarely present at the executive level in proportion to their membership numbers. A notable exception, pointed out to me by the director of the women's division of the East German Unions, the FDGB (Freier Deutscher Gewerkschaftsbund), was the last all-German trade union convention, in 1972, where more than half the delegates were women, a proportional representation corresponding approximately to women's numbers in the labor force. Yet at the same time only three women were on the FDGB executive council, where decisions are really made and agendas for conventions and conferences compiled.

Women's Solidarity

In several countries in very recent years trade union women, an underrepresented minority in their own organizations, have been forming interunion caucuses and study groups, reaching out across jurisdictional lines and organizational exclusiveness to join in discussing grievances and formulating programs on which they can take general action. Some of these alliances extend even across ideological lines, where more than one union center exists within a country. In Sweden and Germany white-collar and blue-collar trade union women work together; in Japan, women of the four trade union federations (left socialist, right socialist, independent, and nonpolitical) coordinate their programs.

In Australia a women's trade union caucus emerged in the early 1970s. In 1973 it held its own convention preceding the national trade union congress and drew up a list of women's demands for presentation to the general assembly. In that country also, two or three of the national unions including the metal workers have set up women's organizations within the regional and local bodies with a view to developing women's sections within the national union. In the United States, the winter of 1973–74 saw the emergence of a national congress of labor union women (CLUW), drawn not only from AFL-CIO unions but from many of the independents as well.

The Auxiliary

Unions in both the East and the West have often sought to catch and hold women's interest and to build it into loyalty to the labor movement by providing programs for women geared specifically to their traditional interests and activities. Structurally the resulting bodies function more like auxiliaries than integral parts of the unions themselves. They serve suppers, organize social activities for themselves and for youths, and, in the case of strikes, run soup kitchens. In the United States some of these auxiliaries have been extremely effective in canvassing and in other grass-roots political activity.

The auxiliary function is perhaps best exemplified in the Israeli Histadrut (the trade union center) where the women's council, Moazet Hapoalot, is made up not only of women trade unionists but of wives of union members. The council carries out the widest range of social activities of any voluntary agency in Israel; it runs child care centers, vacation homes for mothers of large families, educational and vocational programs for women, and community centers for women workers and for housewives. Both inside Israel and outside (where much of the money comes from to finance its activities) it is the counterpart and counterweight to the more middle-class and considerably richer Hadassah and WIZO.

An important function of women's labor publications in the communist countries is to offer advice on child rearing, fashion, recipes, family vacations, and cosmetics.

Women's Issues

Despite attempts to accommodate women's interests into the unions, women leaders in the unions express frustration, sometimes in cynical amusement, sometimes in outright bitterness. The common complaint is that women's issues are not listened to; or, if listened to, not understood; and in no case considered of prime importance. Women's issues may be included on the original list of demands with which a union enters collective bargaining but when no woman is on the bargaining committee to insist upon their retention, they disappear before the hard bargaining begins, traded off at early stages for minor employer concessions.

When the Australian women came before the Trade Union Congress with the report of their caucus sessions, large numbers of male delegates simply left the hall; of those remaining, the majority ostentatiously paid no attention to the women's presentations — either retreating behind newspapers or engaging in audible conversation among themselves. While several of the women's resolutions were routinely adopted, no provision whatever was made for further action. The congress is, for example, on record for improved child care but has no committee, division, or department charged with pursuing its implementation.

West German women in the metal trades union (the largest union in the world) pressed very hard for abolition of the two lowest grades on the pay scale where all but a few women were clustered. They appeared to win victory when Grade I was abolished. It was pyrrhic. Very shortly a new category, Grade XI, appeared at the top of the scale, populated entirely by men. To be sure, everybody including the women at the bottom of the ladder got a raise; the infamous Grade I exists no more. But the differentials still exist and women still occupy the two lowest slots on the scale. The change consists entirely in a sleight of hand — they are numbered not I and II but II and III.

Working Women's Allies

Can trade union women strengthen their position by allying themselves with the larger women's movement in each country? Experience in many places suggests that blue-collar women distrust such alliances, when they consider them at all. Blue-collar workers, whether organized or unorganized, are only occasionally in touch with the so-called women's movement and for the most part have had little sympathy with or understanding of the "liberation" groups. (Australia's Women's Electoral Lobby [WEL] with its committee on working women is an exceptional case.) West Germany, where the unions are a part of the national federation of women's organizations (Das Frauenrat), is also an exception. As a symbol of the unions' significant role in it, the federation's new president is the head of the women's division of the national trade union center. In support of the trade union women's initiative, the *Rat* made the subject of equal pay a special matter of study and action for its affiliates with the result that union women have gained broad understanding and support of their demands for reevaluation of the components of wages.[2]

In Sweden, an informant there remarked, no amount of women's solidarity within the unions or alliance outside was effective in improving Swedish women's trade union status. First the male unionists had to be persuaded to deal with women's problems at their root, namely with the concentration of women in the low-pay categories. It was a long process. The program that emerged under the slogan "solidarity in wage policy" called for awarding the highest wage increases to the lowest-paid workers over a number of years with the result that the male-female pay differentials were substantially narrowed.

In most of the noncommunist countries the male-dominated unions look upon women as a problem group, mainly because they are both hard to organize and, once organized, lethargic in participating in union affairs. They don't come to meetings. They are unwilling to take on jobs as stewards. They have no particular understanding of unions and little loyalty to the movement. They are a dead weight. It is against these preconceptions that women have difficulty in seeking men as allies.

In the communist countries the picture on the surface appears different, but a closer examination discloses similarly that women's roles in the unions are more often acted out in welfare than in economic functions. Under communism, trade unions administer social security and social welfare programs; they are expected to play a significant role in promoting such undertakings as the establishment of sports, recreation, and child care centers at the factories and in workers' residential neighborhoods; and they have oversight of a network of clinics, and vacation and rest homes set up by the factories. These social service functions are very frequently carried out by women activists.

Most communist countries have in addition to the unions a national women's organization made up of women not affiliated either to the unions or to the agricultural organizations. A national women's congress is held from time to time bringing all types of groups together (union, agricultural, and otherwise unassigned women), although congress actions are not binding on the programs of the trade union women.

---

2. See discussion under Equal Pay, chapter 6.

As a matter of course, these women's groups mainly serve the purpose of activating a maximum number of women wherever they are — on the land, in the factories, in the professions, and neighborhood associations — in organizations that will serve as transmission belts to further the aims of the party and the state. Their programs are aimed at varying levels of political development with perhaps the most primitive ones being in the collectives and cooperatives. The union committee within each factory is concerned that sufficient services are provided for women in the plants to enable them to work at their productive best. This function is not only genuinely helpful to women workers but vital for the life of the party and the economic progress of the state.

Everwhere the problem for women as women within the trade unions is their minority position; their lack of representation in the seats of power and decision making; the isolation of their problems and representation in a dependent marginal division; the assignments to them of women's jobs in social service, secretarial chores, and food serving; and the disregard and devaluation of the issues of prime importance to them — child care and equal pay.

XIV. Individual versus Social Responsibility

Although the problems characteristic of mothers at work occur in most countries, women are typically left to solve their problems alone and individually. In fact, the conditions under which women workers function are so endemic in modern industrial societies as to constitute social problems; nevertheless, they are more often treated as individual than as social matters and only exceptionally, fractionally, and irregularly subjected to social solutions.

If we run down the list of circumstances and difficulties discussed so far—the growing number of women and mothers who are working; the pressures on them to work; the problems of reentry into the labor force after interruption of work or career; the limitations on work opportunity and earnings, even among the more highly educated women; the frequent underuse of female talent; the double burden of care for home and attention to work; the shortage in child care; the drawbacks to part-time work; the failure of labor market policy to deal forthrightly with the needs of women; the illusory promise in the equal pay doctrine; the confusion, guilt, and frustration common to working mothers who find themselves unable to cope; the discriminatory effect of much so-called protective legislation and the failure to provide protection and assistance for the childbearing function itself; the minor position accorded women in trade unions — we are impressed not only with the magnitude of the problems but also with their interconnectedness and their mutually enhancing effects. Clearly, coping with them calls for coordination among labor market, social welfare, and educational policy makers.

Learning from Others

The communists, as we have seen, have in fact mobilized most of their womanpower. They recognized that to do so involved the establishment of training, child care, health, educational, and recreational institutions. These have been costed at the expense of the industry or administrative bureaucracy employing women or charged directly to the state (and since all plant profits go to the state, the difference is only one in accounting). But they have not capitalized or operated these institutions at the expense of the individual working woman who is expected to use them.

To be sure, they have done this because they needed every hand, head, and back to develop a modern industrial economy. It is not immediately important to know whether the state enters on these programs out of a commitment to communist concepts of sex equality or to assure full control of childhood training and education or to ensure a maximum of uninterrupted production. The question is rather whether the noncommunist societies after a straightforward recognition of women's special needs, could not for their own reasons do as much — or more.

Yet in the noncommunist countries women are for the most part left to solve their problems alone and single-handedly. We treat these matters as though a woman's decisions to go to work were solely her personal choice, and she alone should carry the responsibility and the expense for the causes and consequences. I would hope that the material brought together here would strongly suggest that we are dealing with a social problem of worldwide dimensions. The single fact that substantially the same range of problems arises whether the society is organized communally or individualistically, whether industry is owned by the state or by private individuals and corporations, whether laws are passed by single-party governments or where parties are in conflict, would seem to furnish presumptive evidence that the circumstances bringing women to the labor market and locating them within it are beyond the control of its individual participants.

Although most countries in this study have taken some cognizance of the working mother in labor market policy, law, social welfare programs, or the educational system, the approaches, with the possible exception of Sweden's, have usually been piecemeal and unrelated. The consequence is that policies meant to be remedial have often at worst canceled one another out and at best proved insufficient.

Even Sweden has not had completely satisfactory results, either in terms of attainment of the labor market goals that have been set or in terms of the numbers of women who have entered the market under the current programs. The very criticism, however, with which the Swedes regard the shortcomings of their government in fulfilling the program is a measure of their commitment to its goals. (The concern with which the ever-cutting editorials on the subject in *Dagens Nyheter,* Sweden's leading daily newspaper, are followed is one recurring indication of how incisively they speak.) The heavy costs of the program were carefully calculated and assumed. The very acceptance of the size of the investment in the program was in itself recognition that these costs are far beyond what individuals can bear personally, to say nothing of the ordinary citizen's power to call up the necessary institutional resources to meet his or her needs. Thus not only is the state assuming a social responsibility for dealing in specific and continuing ways with the adult woman's problems at work, it has found as we noted in chapter 10 that the investment pays off and in the middle run.

Lest there be any misunderstanding about whether Swedish women still have any choice about working, a value that seems to be of central importance in Western countries, the Swedes insist that they too very much want to protect women's own choice about whether to work or not to work. In fact, although their numbers in the labor force increase steadily year by year, the rise is not spectacular. Swedish mothers do not have a higher rate of participation in the labor force than do mothers in other noncommunist countries. What this means, I believe, is that it is not necessary to posit full employment of married women, as the communist countries would like to do, in order to make support programs for working mothers a proper charge on the economy.

A Maternal Bill of Rights

Again let us turn to the United States in our search for an example of what is within the range of the possible.

Following World War II, a grateful nation undertook to make up to its young men, as they were demobilized from the Army, for earnings and training lost when they interrupted their work lives to go to war by adopting the G.I. Bill of Rights. They had for the most part lost the very years which women lose when they leave the labor force for months or years to have children—incidentally, a service to society incomparably more necessary and useful than the sacrifices war demands of men.

Is it not possible to think of a maternal bill of rights?

Such a bill would recognize that the interruption of work is in the service of the country; that it is an interruption most women routinely take; that the interruption is simply that—a hiatus between employment and employment; that such interruptions cannot take place without some loss of skill and productivity, and the forgoing of acquaintance with the ever-constant introduction of new materials, processes, machines, tools, and techniques.

A maternal bill of rights could offer women the means for continuing or taking up vocational or general education. It would be tailored first to man-power needs and within that range to individual predilections. It could allow for a reassessment of earlier work and educational experience so as to permit a fresh start or it could refresh old skills for updated functions. A detail in planning would permit women to carry on some of this training part time while they were still mainly occupied with child care and thus to cut short somewhat the time needed for full-time training at reentry. It could be linked to the unemployment insurance system in such a way that covered work experience before the "interruption" could be carried forward to ensure support during training that had received the approval of the labor market specialists.

It could contain, as Veterans' Administration programs have done, ample counseling and guidance services covering the period not only of training but of the early months of work and of necessary periods of "adjustment" (in the Swedish sense) in the course of employment.

It could provide subsidies to employers to pay the cost of on-the-job training or related off-the-job training to fit selected individuals for higher-skilled jobs and equip them for promotional opportunities.

It would not be built around residential job-training camps at locations distant from women's homes, but rather linked to established facilities in and near their communities. The new community college system now widely spread across the United States offers an almost ideal institutional setting. These colleges are already closely integrated with industrial and educational facilities in their localities. They are prepared to train for existing jobs as well as to offer general education at junior-college level for persons aspiring to academic and professional careers. Most of them are prepared to admit adults for either part-time or full-time instruction. They are new, growing, flexible, locally oriented, relatively inexpensive institutions.

Investments in child care will have to go hand in hand with training. Programs that will genuinely serve child development and meet the needs of working mothers call for national standard setting and federal subsidy. Programs that will serve the country cannot be financed individually, least of all by unskilled and semiskilled blue- and white-collar women working at low rates of pay. Like public schooling, preschooling must be financed with a mixture of public resources.

It is surely not merely visionary to believe that under programs such as these women's work experience would take on new meaning for them, with positive results for their performance as workers and for their personal satisfaction with work.

Conclusion

Married women are in the labor market to stay. At present they are severely victimized there, mainly because their work-life cycle differs radically from that of men. Society could recognize this fact and devise accommodations to it that might well pay off in productive terms and in reward to women as individuals.

Working mothers carry a double burden of home and child care duties on the one hand and employment on the other. Immediate provision of child care facilities and opportunities for part-time work would greatly ease these burdens, until society accommodates over the long run to new definitions of sex roles and equalization of parental responsibilities.

The problems women face are so numerous and so widespread as to reflect both the injustice of expecting them to be able to handle them individually and the need to move rapidly toward social solutions. The experiences of a number of countries, both communist and noncommunist, suggest a variety of ways for dealing with these problems. The institution of such programs could result in maximizing women's productivity and earnings and minimizing the heavy burdens that they bear in every country.

Bibliography

Adams, Arvil V. *Toward Fair Employment and the EEOC: A Final Report.* Washington, D.C.: Research Division, U.S. Equal Opportunity Commission, August 31, 1972.

Bell, Carolyn Shaw. "Women and Social Security: Contributions and Benefits." Paper prepared for the hearings of the Joint Economic Committee on the economic problems of women, July 25, 1973.

Berent, Jerzy. "Some Demographic Aspects of Female Employment in Eastern Europe and the USSR." *International Labour Review* 101, no. 2 (February 1970): 175–92.

Bericht über die Situation der Frau in Oesterreich [Report on the situation of women in Austria]. Section 5: "Die Frau im Beruf" [The woman at work]. Vienna: Bundes-kanzleramt, 1975.

Borris, Maria. *Die Benachteiligung der Maedchen in Schulen der Bundesrepublik und Westberlin* [The disadvantagement of girls in schools in the Federal Republic ...u West Berlin]. Frankfurt-am-Main: Europaeischer Verlagsanstalt, 1972.

Chinoy, Eli. *The Auto Worker and the American Dream.* Garden City, N.Y.: Doubleday, 1955.

Cole, G. D. H. *A Short History of the English Working Class Movement, 1789–1947.* London: Allen & Unwin, 1947.

Cook, Alice H. "Maternity Benefits." U.S. National Committee, the International Society for Labor Law and Social Legislation, *Bulletin* 8, no. 3 (October 1975).

Dodge, Norton T. *Women in the Soviet Economy.* Baltimore: Johns Hopkins Press, 1966.

"EEOC Says It Has Filed 198 Title VII Suits against Firms and Unions." Bureau of National Affairs, *Daily Labor Report,* no. 93 (May 13, 1974):A2.

Ferge, Susan. "Hungary." In *Child Care—Who Cares?,* edited by Pamela Roby. New York: Harper & Row, 1973.

Feshbach, Murray, and Stephen Rapawy. "Labor Constraints in the Five Year Plan." In *Soviet Economic Prospects for the Seventies,* a compendium of papers submitted to the U.S. Congress Joint Economic Committee, 93d Cong., 1st Sess., June 27, 1973.

Fishelson, Gideon. "Intensity of Participation in the Labor Force of Married Women." Mimeographed. Israel: University of Tel Aviv, August 1971.

Fogarty, Michael P., Rhona Rapoport, and Robert N. Rapoport. *Sex, Career and Family: Including an International Review of Women's Roles.* Beverly Hills, Calif.: Sage, 1971.

Galenson, Marjorie. *Women and Work: An International Comparison.* Ithaca: New York State School of Industrial and Labor Relations, Cornell University, 1973.

Goralnik, A. "Vocational Training." In "Study Tour on Programmes for the Education of Adults, February–March, 1971." Mimeographed. Haifa: Mount Carmel International Training Centre for Community Services.

Great Britain. Department of Employment. *Women and Work: A Statistical Survey.* Manpower Paper No. 9. London: Her Majesty's Stationery Office, 1974.

Grotberg, Edith H., ed. *Day Care: Resources for Decisions.* Washington, D.C.: Office of Economic Opportunity, 1971.

Hallaire, Jean. *Part-time Employment: Its Extent and Its Problems.* Paris: Organisation for Economic Cooperation and Development, 1968.

Harburger, Perez F. "Vocational Education in Israel." Mimeographed. Jerusalem: Ministry of Labor, March 1967.

Hayghe, Howard. "Marital and Family Characteristics of the Labor Force, March 1975." Special Labor Force Report. *Monthly Labor Review* 98, no. 11 (November 1975): 52–56.

Hoskins, Dalmer, and Lenore Bixby. "Women and Social Security: Study of the Situation in Five Countries." *International Social Security Review* 26, nos. 1–2 (1973):75–133.

International Labour Organisation. *Yearbook of Labour Statistics, 1976.* Geneva: ILO, 1976.

Kammer fuer Arbeiter und Angestellte fuer Wien. "Leitfaden fuer die berufstaetige Mutter: Was tue ich, wenn ... ?" [Handbook for the working mother: What do I do when ... ?] Ministry of Labor, 1970, with mimeographed notes on revisions of labor laws, as of January 1, 1973.

Kerr, Clark. "Labor's Income Share and the Labor Movement." In *Unions, Management, and the Public,* edited by E. Wight Bakke, Clark Kerr, and Charles W. Anrod. 3d ed. New York: Harcourt Brace, 1967.

_____. "Trade Unionism and Distributive Shares." In *Readings in Labor Economics and Labor Relations,* edited by Richard L. Rowan and Herbert R. Northrup. Homewood, Ill.: Irwin, 1968.

Kharchev, A., and Serge Golod. "Recommendations of the Symposium on Women's Employment and the Family." Minsk, June 21–24, 1969. *Soviet Review* 14, no. 4 (winter 1973–74). More details on the same research are in *Berufstaetige Frau und Familie* [The working woman and the family] (East Berlin: Dietz Verlag, 1972); and "The Two Roles of Russian Working Women in an Urban Area," in Andrée Michel, *Family Issues of Employed Women in Europe and America* (Leiden: E. J. Brill, 1971).

Labour Canada. Women's Bureau. *Women in the Labour Force: Facts and Figures 1975.* Ottawa: Information Canada, 1975.

Landsorganisationen i Sverige. *The Trade Unions and the Family: A Report by the LO Council for Family Questions.* Stockholm: Prisma, 1970.

Lapidus, Gail Warshofsky. "USSR Women at Work: Changing Patterns." *Industrial Relations* 14, no. 2 (May 1975):178–95.

Laroque, Pierre. "Women's Rights and Widows' Pensions." *International Labour Review* 106 (July 1972):1–10.

Liljeström, Rita. *Sex Roles in Transition.* Stockholm: Swedish Institute, 1975.

Mandel, William M. *Soviet Woman.* Garden City, N.Y.: Anchor Books, 1975.

Meyer, Thomas, and Ruth Crummererl. "Berufliche Ausbildung in Industrie und Handwerk in Hessen" [Vocational training in industry and handcrafts in Hesse]. *Zur Situation im Lande Hessen,* vol. 1. Wiesbaden: Hessische Landesentwicklungs — und Treuhandgesellschaft, 1972.

Myrdal, Alva. "Towards Equality." Report to the Swedish Social Democratic Party. Stockholm: Prisma, 1971.

Myrdal, Alva, and Viola Klein. *Women's Two Roles: Home and Work.* London: Routledge and Paul, 1956.

Official Yearbook of Australia, 1974. Canberra: Australian Bureau of Statistics, 1975.

Organisation for Economic Cooperation and Development. *Employment of Women.* Regional Trade Union Seminar, Paris, November 26–29, 1968. Paris: OECD, 1970.

———. "The Role of Women in the Economy: Japan." Mimeographed. National Report, September 1973.

———. "The Role of Women in the Economy: Sweden." Mimeographed. National Report, March 1973.

"Pregnancy May Be Excluded from Health and Disability Coverage: General Electric Co. v. Gilbert, U.S. Supreme Court, Dec. 7, 1976." *Womanpower 7,* no. 1 (January 1977):5–7.

Pross, Helge. *Gleichberechtigung im Beruf? Eine Untersuchung mit 7,000 Arbeitnehmerinnen in der EWG* [Equality in work? A study of 7,000 women workers in the EEC]. Frankfurt: Athenaeum Verlag, 1973.

Rosengren, Bodil. "More Time for the Children: A Survey of Recent Developments in the Care of Young Children." Mimeographed. *Current Sweden* 131 (October 1976).

———. *Pre-School in Sweden.* Stockholm: Swedish Institute, 1973.

Ross, Susan D. "Sex Discrimination and 'Protective' Labor Legislation." Hearings before the Special Subcommittee on Education and Labor, House of Representatives, 91st Cong., 2d Sess. Part 1, June 17–30, 1970.

Sacks, Michael Paul. *Women's Work in Soviet Russia: Continuity in the Midst of Change.* New York: Praeger, 1976.

St. George, George. *Our Soviet Sister.* Washington, D.C.: Robert B. Luce, 1973.

Sawhill, Isabel. "The Economics of Discrimination against Women: Some New Findings." *Journal of Human Resources* 8, no. 3 (Summer 1973): 383–95.

Seear, B. N. *Re-entry of Women to the Labour Market after an Interruption in Employment.* Paris: Organisation for Economic Cooperation and Development, 1971.

Sommerkorn, Ingrid, R. Nave-Herz, and Christine Kulke. "Women's Careers: Experience from East and West Germany." *PEP (Political and Economic Planning)* Broadsheet 36, no. 520 (October 1970).

"Speakers Probe Sex Bias at ABA Labor Relations Meeting." Bureau of National Affairs, *Daily Labor Report,* no. 92 (May 10, 1974): A7.

Statistical Abstract of Israel, 1973. Jerusalem: Central Bureau of Statistics, 1973.

Statistisches Handbuch für die Republik Oesterreich, 1975. Vienna: Statistisches Zentralamt, 1975.

Statistisches Jahrbuch der Deutschen Demokratischen Republik, 1976. Berlin: Staatsverlag der DDR, 1976.

Statistisches Jahrbuch für die Bundesrepublik Deutschland, 1976. Wiesbaden: Statistisches Bundesamt, 1976.

Statistisk årbok for Norge: 1976. Oslo: Statistisk Sentralbyrå, 1976.

Statistisk Årsbok för Sverige, 1976. Stockholm: Statistiska Centralbyrån, 1976.

The Status of Women in Sweden. Report of the Swedish Government to the United Nations. Stockholm: Swedish Institute, 1968.

Sullerot, Evelyne. *Women, Society, and Change.* London: World University Library, Weidenfeld and Nicolson, 1971.

Suter, Larry E., and Herman P. Miller. "Components of Income Differences between Men and Career Women." *American Journal of Sociology* 78, no. 4 (January 1973): 962–74.

"The Swedish Population." *Fact Sheets on Sweden,* June 1976.

Szalai, Alexander, ed. *Use of Time: A Multinational Study.* Paris: Mouton, 1972.

Turchaninova, Svetlana. "Trends in Women's Employment in the USSR." *International Labour Review* 112, no. 4 (October 1975): 253–64.

United Nations. "Seminar on the Participation of Women in the Economic Life of Their Countries." Moscow, USSR, September 8–21, 1970. Organized by the UN Division of Human Rights.

U.S. Bureau of the Census. "Consumer Income." *Current Population Reports,* Series P-60, no. 101 (January 1976).

U.S. Department of Labor, Bureau of Labor Statistics. *Employment and Earnings* 24, no. 5 (May 1977).

U.S. Supreme Court. "Decision of Supreme Court in Geduldig v. Aiello, et al." *Daily Labor Report,* no. 117 (June 17, 1974): D1–D7.

U.S. Supreme Court. "Decision of Supreme Court in International Brotherhood of Teamsters v. United States and Equal Employment Opportunity Commission." *Daily Labor Report,* no. 105 (May 31, 1977): D8.

U.S. Women's Bureau. *Handbook on Women Workers.* Bulletin 294. Washington, D.C.: GPO, 1969.

_____. *1975 Handbook on Women Workers.* Bulletin 297. Washington, D.C.: GPO, 1976.

U.S. Women's Bureau and the Japanese Women's and Minors' Bureau. *The Role and Status of Women Workers in the United States and Japan.* Washington, D.C.: GPO, 1976.

Vangsnes, Kari. "Equal Pay in Norway." *International Labour Review* 103, no. 4 (April 1971): 379–92.

Walker, Kathryn, and William H. Gauger. *The Dollar Value of Household Work.* Social Sciences, Consumer Economics and Public Policy No. 5, Information Bulletin 60. Ithaca: New York State College of Human Ecology, Cornell University, June 1973.

Womanpower (monthly newsletter on equal opportunity for women) 6, no. 11 (November 1976): 4–5. [*Womanpower* is a source of current information on court decisions and legislation.]

Yearbook of Nordic Statistics, 1976. Stockholm: Nordic Council, 1977.

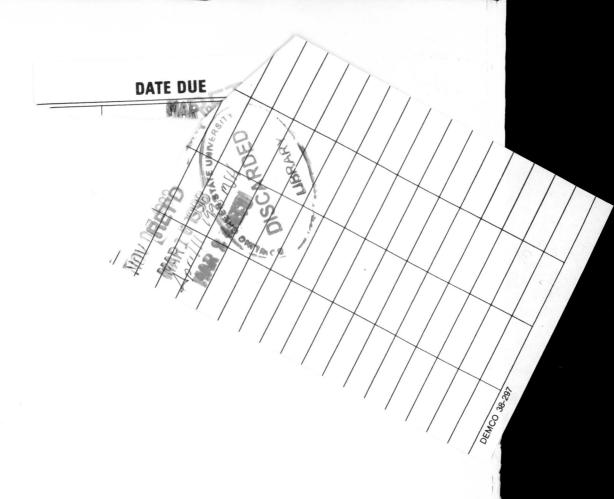